D1577941

$\mathcal{F}$LOWERS *and* $\mathcal{T}$REES
OF THE
TRINITY ALPS

a photographic guide

photography and text by

ALICE GOEN JONES

published by
THE TRINITY COUNTY HISTORICAL SOCIETY
Weaverville, California

Copyright © 1986 by Alice Goen Jones
All rights reserved
Library of Congress Card Number 86-50366
ISBN #0-9607054-2-2
Published in 1986 by Trinity County Historical Society
  in Weaverville, California
Typography and design
  by Golden State Printers, Weaverville, California
Printed in United States of America
  by Intercollegiate Press, Shawnee, Kansas

Contents

REFERENCES

A California Flora and Supplement,
by Phillip A. Munz, 1968

A Manual of the Flowering Plants of California,
by Willis Linn Jepson, 1925

Forest Trees of the Pacific Slope,
by George B. Sudworth, 1908

A Flora of the Trinity Alps of Northern California,
by William J. Ferlatta, 1974

An Illustrated Manual of California Shrubs,
by Howard E. McMinn, 1939

Wildflowers of Western America,
by Robert T. and Margaret C. Orr, 1974

Wildflowers of the Pacific Coast,
by Leslie L. Haskin, 1977

The Wildflowers of California,
by Mary Elizabeth Parsons, 1966

Wildflowers 3,
by Elizabeth L. Horn, 1976

Wildflowers of the United States. Vol V,
The Northwestern States,
by Harold William Rickett, Publication of
the New York Botanical Garden, 1971

Field Guide to North American Wildflowers,
Western Region,
by the National Audubon Society, 1985

ACKNOWLEDGEMENTS

The following photos were taken by
Will Challis

17. LACE-POD
19. WILD CUCUMBER
122. PURDY'S SEDUM
170. FIRE-CRACKER FLOWER
200. SHOWY PHLOX
255. BLUE GENTIAN

Lucille Kibbee

23. BLACK LAUREL
175. PINK MOUNTAIN HEATHER

The author wishes to gratefully
acknowledge the use of these photos
as they make a valuable contribution
to this collection.

FOREWORD

It was in 1950 that the author moved to Weaverville in Trinity County, California, where her husband was to serve as U.S. Forest Service District Ranger for an area embracing the heart of the Trinity Alps. For the next 35 years she had ample opportunity to come to know and love these mountains well, spending countless hours hiking the trails and photographing the flowers.

Alice Jones is a botanist and forester with degrees in botany and forestry from the University of California at Los Angeles and the University of California at Berkeley, respectively. With this as a background and with serious photography as a hobby it was natural that she should accumulate a botanical and photographic collection of the plants of the area. With encouragement from friends she decided to share her collection with others by developing this photographic guide to the flowers and trees growing in this very unique part of California.

The author's interest extends beyond the natural history of the area to include the rich and colorful history of Trinity County. For nearly 20 years she has been on the Board of Directors of the Trinity County Historical Society and for two terms served as its president. Because of this dedication she offered to make this book available to the Society. Her offer was accepted and all proceeds from the sale of this book are being used by the Society for its work in the management and development of the J.J. Jackson Memorial Museum in Weaverville.

It is the author's wish that all those who read this book will find joy in becoming more intimately familiar with the many, many plants that clothe these mountains.

Trinity County Historical Society

INTRODUCTION/how to use this book

This is a collection of 332 photos of flowers and trees growing in the Trinity Alps and adjacent areas of the Klamath Mountains of northwestern California. This is a complex and unique botanical region. Represented here are species growing in diverse ecological zones ranging from the Ponderosa-Digger Pine plant community at 2000' near Weaverville to sub-alpine plants growing at nearly 9000' on the slopes of Thompson Peak and Mt. Eddy. Although this collection represents but a fraction of the species that grow in these mountains it does include a large portion of the plants which would be most apt to be noticed by a visitor to the region. The majority of the photographs were taken within the boundaries of the Trinity Alps Wilderness Area.

Although emphasis has been placed on the wildflowers some of the more common trees and shrubs have been included in a separate section. Flower photos have been grouped in sections by color. It should be noted that the color of a flower is often variable within a species and the category in which it is found in this book may differ from the color of the specimen that the reader may have observed. For example, a lavender flower may be more pinkish than bluish or might be more whitish than lavender thus placing it in a different section. It should also be remembered that photo reproductions do not always display color accurately. This is especially true in the case of blue flowers. If there is a question regarding color, refer to the descriptive text which follows the photo section. Note should also be made of the supplemental lists appearing in the front of each color section.

A descriptive text is provided for each species. The descriptions in this text section are not intended to be considered complete descriptions. Instead, emphasis is given to those significant characteristics which, if present, should help the layman confirm identifications he may have made from the photos. Care has been taken to avoid the use of technical terms whenever possible. It has, however, been necessary to use some general botanical terms. To assist in the understanding of these terms an illustrated glossary is provided. Included with the description of each plant is the area in which the photo was taken as well as other areas in which the plant has been observed. The month the photo was taken is also noted as well as the type of habitat in which the plant grows.

It should be remembered that common names are extremely variable with the same name often applied to more than one species. Likewise, a single species may have more than one common name applied to it. The common names appearing in this book should, therefore, be considered to be but one of possibly several acceptable names. In order, however, for this collection to have some scientific merit a specific botanical name is included. In a few cases this scientific name may be subject to question as identification was not always possible in the field. Carrying heavy reference books on botanical hikes and backpack trips was not always practical and identification had to be made at a later time from the photograph, a herbarium specimen, or even from casual observation and memory. The identifications made, however, are sufficiently accurate to serve as satisfactory identifications for the layman and for general purposes.

A list of reference books used is provided. For the purposes of this book the nomenclature used by Munz is largely followed. There are a few cases where the nomenclature used by Jepson, Rickett, or Ferlatta was preferred.

SECTION I

flowers that are white, whitish, cream, or greenish-white

9

1. POISON OAK

2. ELK'S CLOVER (fruit)

3. WHITE BRODIAEA

4. ELK'S CLOVER (flower)

5. DUTCHMAN'S PIPE

6. SHOWY STICKSEED

7. INSIDE-OUT FLOWER

8. INDIAN CARTWHEEL
or STRINGFLOWER

9. STARWORT

10. PEARLY EVERLASTING

11. BALLHEAD SANDWORT

12. NUTTALL'S SANDWORT

13. FIELD CHICKWEED

14. YARROW

15. WESTERN COLTSFOOT

16. FRINGE-BRACT THISTLE

17. LACE POD

18. PENNY CRESS

19. HILL MAN-ROOT or WILD CUCUMBER

20. OX-EYE DAISY

21. PINE-MAT MANZANITA

22. LABRADOR TEA

3. BLACK LAUREL

24. WHITE HEATHER

25. FEW-FLOWERED
BLEEDING HEART

26. WESTERN AZALEA

27. CATERPILLAR PLANT

28. DWARF HESPERIOCHIRON

29. GROUND IRIS

30. SPANISH CLOVER

31. LONG-STALKED CLOVER

32. SISKIYOU LOCOWEED
or BALLOON PLANT

33. BRIDE'S BONNET or CLINTONIA

34. PUSSY EARS

35. FAIRY BELLS
(flower)

36. FAIRY BELLS
(fruit)

37. FAWN LILY

38. BEAR GRASS

39. TWISTED STALK

40. CORN-LILY or FALSE HELLEBORE

41. GREENBRIER

42. CASCADE LILY

43. STAR-FLOWER

44. WESTERN SOLOMON'S SEAL

45. COMMON TRILLIUM

46. WESTERN TOLFIELDIA

47. WHITE-FLOWERED SCHOENOLIRION

48. WESTERN TRILLIUM

49. DEATH CAMAS

50. BOG REIN-ORCHID

51. SLENDER PHLOX

52. NUTTALL'S LINANTHUS

53. PHANTOM ORCHID

54. CALIFORNIA LADY SLIPPER

55. COMPOSITE BUCKWHEAT

56. NEEDLE-LEAVED
NAVARRETIA

WHITISH

57. NEVADA LEWISIA

58. KNOTWEED

59. NAKED STEM BUCKWHEAT

60. THREE-LEAVED LEWISIA

61. FROSTED MINER'S LETTUCE

62. MINER'S LETTUCE

63. SIBERIAN MONTIA

64. ONE-SIDED WINTERGREEN

65. INDIAN PIPE

66. WHITE-VEINED SHINLEAF

67. BUCKBRUSH

68. DRUMMOND'S ANEMONE

69. WESTERN PASQUE FLOWER
or MOUNTAIN ANEMONE

70. MOUNTAIN
WHITETHORN

71. WOOD ANEMONE

72. MARSH MARIGOLD

73. SNOWBRUSH

74. COFFEEBERRY

75. NINE-BARK

76. WOOD STRAWBERRY

77. THIMBLEBERRY

78. DUSKY HORKELIA

79. SERVICEBERRY

80. OCEAN SPRAY

81. GRAY'S BEDSTRAW

82. SWEET BEDSTRAW

83. WILD CURRANT

84. MOUNTAIN BOYKINIA

86. ALUM ROOT

85. GRASS-OF-PARNASSUS

88. WOODLAND STAR

87. INDIAN RHUBARB

89. LEAFY LOUSEWORT

90. SNOWDROP BUSH

91. YERBA DE SELVA

92. YAMPAH

93. CALIFORNIA LOVAGE

94. ANGELICA

95. COW-PARSNIP

96. MACLOSKEY'S VIOLET

SECTION II

flowers that are yellow,
yellowish, or orange

97. GOLDEN BRODIAEA

98. ORANGE HONEYSUCKLE

99. ORANGE-FLOWERED AGOSERIS

100. MOUNTAIN ARNICA

101. RABBIT BRUSH

102. WOOLY SUNFLOWER

103. HOUNDSTONGUE HAWKWEED

104. ROCK DAISY

105. CALIFORNIA
    LITTLE SUNFLOWER

106. BIGELOW SNEEZEWEED

107. COMMON MADIA

108. GUM PLANT

109. CALIFORNIA
CONE-FLOWER

110. ARROWLEAF SENECIO

111. SINGLE-STEMMED BUTTERWEED

112. MULE-EARS

113. ALPINE GOLDENROD

114. MEADOW GOLDENROD

115. RAILLARDELLA

116. HAWKSBEARD

117. SALSIFY

118. SIERRA WALLFLOWER

119. DYER WOAD

120. WESTERN WALLFLOWER

121. STONECROP

122. PURDY'S SEDUM

123. KLAMATH WEED

124. GOLDEN-EYED GRASS

125. MEADOW LOTUS

126. HILL LOTUS

127. FALSE LUPINE

128. YELLOW FAWN LILY

129. BOG-ASPHODEL

130. YELLOW LUPINE

131. CHECKER-LILY

132. BLAZING STAR

133. BROOM-RAPE

134. BUSH POPPY

135. CALIFORNIA POPPY

136. SULPHUR FLOWER

137. SHRUBBY CINQUEFOIL

38. WATER PLANTIAN BUTTERCUP

139. STICKY CINQUEFOIL

140. IVESIA

142. SAXIFRAGE

141. BIRD'S FOOT BUTTERCUP

144 PRIMROSE MIMULUS

143. COMMON MONKEY-FLOWER

145. COBWEBBY INDIAN PAINT-BRUSH

146. HAIRY PRIMROSE MIMULUS

147. CANDELABRUM MONKEY-FLOWER

148. MUSK FLOWER

149. HOT-ROCK PENSTEMON

150. COMMON MULLEIN

151. SIERRA SANICLE

152. YELLOW OWL'S CLOVER
    or CUTLEAF ORTHOCARPUS

153. STREAM VIOLET

154. MOUNTAIN VIOLET

155. SHELTON'S VIOLET

156. PINE VIOLET

*The following species may
also be pinkish or partially pink
or red in color. They are
described in other sections:*

15. WESTERN COLTSFOOT
25. FEW-FLOWERED BLEEDING HEART
26. WESTERN AZALEA
28. DWARF HESPEROCHIRON
30. SPANISH CLOVER
42. CASCADE LILY
48. WESTERN TRILLIUM
51. SLENDER PHLOX
57. NEVADA LEWISIA
59. NAKED STEM BUCKWHEAT
60. THREE-LEAVED LEWISIA
63. SIBERIAN MONTIA
78. DUSKY HORKELIA
83. WILD CURRANT
87. INDIAN RHUBARB
88. WOODLAND STAR
199. SPREADING PHLOX
239. JESSICA'S STICKSEED
309. HAZELNUT

SECTION III

flowers that are pink, red
or brownish-red

157. MOUNTAIN DOGBANE

158. PURPLE MILKWEED

159. COMMON MILKWEED

160. SWAMP ONION

161. SCYTHE-LEAVED ONION

162. FIRE-CRACKER FLOWER

163. WESTERN HOUND'S TONGUE

164. TWINFLOWER

165. CREEPING SNOWBERRY (fruit)

166. COMMON SNOWBERRY

167. MOUNTAIN DAISY
   or DAISY FLEABANE

168. ROSY EVERLASTING

169. INDIAN CARTWHEEL
or STRINGFLOWER

170. WILD GINGER

171. BREWER'S THISTLE

172. BULL THISTLE

173. ANDERSON'S THISTLE

174. TOOTHWORT or MILK-MAIDS

175. PINK MOUNTAIN HEATHER

176. GREENLEAF
MANZANITA

177. BLEEDING HEART

178. REDBUD

179. BROAD-LEAVED LOTUS

180. SHASTA CLOVER

181. SCARLET FRITILLARY

182. GIANT HYSSOP

183. LEOPARD LILY

184. ROSE EPILOBIUM
or ROCK FRINGE

185. RED ELDERBERRY (fruit)

186. OREGON SIDALCEA

187. STRIPED CORAL-ROOT

188. CALYPSO ORCHID

190. CLARKIA or RED RIBBONS

189. SPOTTED CORAL ROOT

192. STREAM ORCHID

91. CALIFORNIA GROUND CONE

193. FIREWEED

194. NARROW-LEAVED COLLOMIA

195. BRIGHT COLLOMIA

196. VARIABLE-LEAVED COLLOMIA

197. LARGE-FLOWERED COLLOMIA

198. WILLOW-HERB

199. SPREADING PHLOX

200. SHOWY PHLOX

201. HENDERSON'S SHOOTING STAR

202. JEFFREY'S SHOOTING STAR

203. DWARF MINER'S LETTUCE

204. PUSSY PAWS

205. SISKIYOU LEWISIA

206. COLUMBIA LEWISIA

207. LEE'S LEWISIA

208. SCARLET GILIA

209. STAR-FLOWER

210. SIERRA PRIMROSE

211. PINE-DROPS

212. LITTLE PRINCE'S PINE

214. MILKWORT

213. LEAFLESS PYROLA

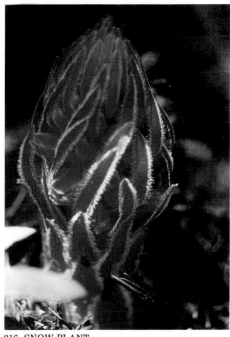

216. SNOW-PLANT

215. PIPSISSEWA or PRINCE'S PINE

217. SUGAR STICK

218. RED COLUMBINE

219. RED LARKSPUR

220. DOUGLAS SPIRAEA

221. CALIFORNIA PITCHER PLANT
  (flower)

222. CALIFORNIA PITCHER PLANT
  (leaves)

223. MOUNTAIN SPIRAEA

224. LAYNE'S MONKEY-FLOWER

225. SIERRA GOOSEBERRY

226. LITTLE ELEPHANT'S HEAD

227. MOUNTAIN PRIDE

228. LEWIS MONKEY-FLOWER

229. INDIAN WARRIOR

230. WAVY-LEAVED INDIAN PAINT-BRUSH

231. COPELAND'S OWL'S CLOVER

232. GREAT RED INDIAN
PAINT-BRUSH

SECTION IV

flowers that are bluish, purple, or lavender

233. NARROW-LEAVED MILKWEED

234. OOKOW

235. ELEGANT BRODIAEA

236. HARVEST BRODIAEA

237. CASCADE OREGON GRAPE (fruit)

238. HOUND'S TONGUE

239. JESSICA'S STICKSEED

240. WILKIN'S HAREBELL

241. CASCADE DOWINGEA

242. CALIFORNIA HAREBELL

243. CHICORY

244. SPREADING FLEABANE

246. CASCADE ASTER

245. WESTERN MOUNTAIN ASTER

248. BLUE-VEINED NEMOPHILA

247. ALPINE ASTER

249. MOUNTAIN SHIELDLEAF

250. YERBA SANTA

251. SQUAW LETTUCE or
     CALIFORNIA WATERLEAF

252. DRAPERIA

253. SPOTTED FRITILLARY

254. BLUE-EYED GRASS

255. GREEN GENTIAN

256. BLUE GENTIAN

257. MOUNTAIN PENNYROYAL

258. PALE PENNYROYAL

259. WESTERN BLUE FLAX

260. HEDGE-NETTLE

262. CREEPING SAGE

261. SELF-HEAL

263. AMERICAN VETCH

264. SNAPDRAGON SKULLCAP

265. LYALL'S LUPINE

266. BROAD-LEAVED LUPINE

267. SICKLE-KEELED LUPINE

268. CAMAS

269. STAR TULIP

270. NAKED BROOM-RAPE

271. SQUAW CARPET

272. DWARF CEANOTHUS

273. BLUE FIELD GILIA

274. DWARF LARKSPUR

275. DEER BRUSH

276. LEMMON'S CEANOTHUS

277. TALL MOUNTAIN LARKSPUR

278. MONKSHOOD

279. BLUE PENSTEMON or
GAY PENSTEMON

280. TORREY'S BLUE-EYED MAR

281. DELICATE BLUE-EYED MARY

282. LARGE-FLOWERED BLUE-EYED MARY

283. PARISH'S NIGHTSHADE

284. COPELAND'S SPEEDWELL
or VERONICA

286. SMALL-FLOWERED PENSTEMON

285. WHORLED PENSTEMON

287. COMMON VERBENA

288. SISKIYOU PENSTEMON

The following species are shrubs
that could have been
included in this section. They
are described in other sections:

178. REDBUD
185. RED ELDERBERRY

SECTION V

trees and tall shrubs

289. BIG-LEAF MAPLE
(leaves)

290. BIG-LEAF MAPLE
(flower and fruit)

291. MADRONE (flower)

292. MADRONE (bark)

293. MOUNTAIN DOGWOOD (fruit)

294. MOUNTAIN DOGWOOD (flower)

295. CREEK DOGWOOD (flower)

296. BLACK-FRUIT DOGWOOD
      (fruit)

297. CALIFORNIA BLACK OAK (leaves)

298. CALIFORNIA BLACK OAK (trunk)

299. OREGON WHITE OAK
    (tree)

300. BREWER OAK
    (leaves)

301. SHRUB TAN OAK
 (leaves, acorn, catkins)

302. SADLER OAK (leaves and acorn)

303. BUSH CHINQUAPIN
 (leaves and bur)

304. HUCKLEBERRY OAK
 (leaves and acorn)

306. QUAKING ASPEN (leaves)

305. CALIFORNIA BUCKEYE
(flowers)

307. MOUNTAIN ASH
(fruit)

308. BITTER CHERRY
(flowers)

309. HAZELNUT (staminate flowers)

310. HAZELNUT (pistillate flower)

311. BLACK COTTONWOOD
   (leaves)

312. WESTERN CHOKECHERRY
   (flowers)

313. PONDEROSA PINE (bark)

314. PONDEROSA PINE (tree)

315. JEFFREY PINE (needles)

316. JEFFREY PINE (tree)

318. WESTERN WHITE PINE (needles)

317. SUGAR PINE (trunk)

320. FOXTAIL PINE (needles and cones)

319. FOXTAIL PINE (tree)

321. DIGGER PINE (tree)

322. DIGGER PINE (needles)

323. LODGEPOLE PINE
(needles and cone)

324. YEW (needles and fruit)

325. WHITE FIR (tree)

326. RED FIR (tree with cones)

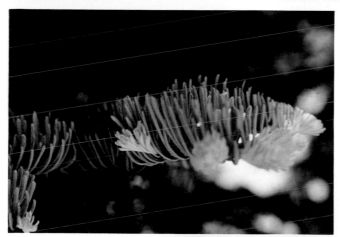

327. RED FIR (needles)

328. DOUGLAS FIR
(needles and cones)

329. MOUNTAIN HEMLOCK (cones)

330. MOUNTAIN HEMLOCK (tree)

331. WEEPING SPRUCE (needles)

332. INCENSE CEDAR (tree)

The descriptions included in this text section are not intended to be considered complete descriptions of the plant. Included here are those significant features which, if present, should help confirm identifications made from the photos. Numbers are the same as those on the corresponding photos.

SPECIES DESCRIPTIONS

1. POISON OAK
Rhus diversiloba
Habitat: dry rocky slopes

SUMAC FAMILY
Anacardiaceae
May

This erect and spreading shrub can sometimes be vine-like on the trunks of trees. Its leaves have 3, often shiny, leaflets 1"-4" long with irregularly lobed edges. The inconspicuous greenish-white flowers bloom in a loose panicle shortly after the leaves appear in the spring. The plant juices (an oil) are highly irritating to the skin.
Type locality: French Creek

2. ELK'S CLOVER (fruit)
Aralia californica
For description see #4.

3. WHITE BRODIAEA
Brodiaea hyacinthina
Habitat: moist or dry meadows

AMARYLLIS FAMILY
Amaryllidaceae
June

This plant has erect open clusters of bowl-shaped flowers growing in an umbel at the end of simple slender stems 1'-1½' tall. The individual blossoms are up to ½" long with petal-like flower segments that are white and have a greenish or bluish vein in the middle.
Type locality: Parker Meadow, Norwegian Meadow

4. ELK'S CLOVER
Aralia californica
Habitat: moist shaded canyons and streamsides

ARALIA FAMILY
Araliaceae
July

Although from 6'-10' tall this plant is not a shrub. It is an herb having large leaves that are divided into 3 segments, each of which are again divided into 3-5 large leaflets up to 8" long. A loosely branched flower cluster over 12" long contains numerous small umbels of tiny white flowers which develop into black berries 1/8" in diameter (see #2).
Type locality: Boulder Creek, Stuart's Fork

5. DUTCHMAN'S PIPE — BIRTHWORT FAMILY

Aristolochia californica — *Aristolochiaceae*

Habitat: near streambanks at lower elevations — March

This is a woody vine 8'-12' long which climbs over other plants and has flowers that appear before the leaves have fully developed. The flowers are greenish with purple veins and resemble the bowl of an old-fashioned smoking pipe as they hang pendulous from the axils of small branchlets. They are 1"-1½" long. The leaves are up to 6" long and somewhat heart-shaped.

Type locality: Lower Clear Creek

6. SHOWY STICKSEED — BORAGE FAMILY

Hackelia bella — *Boraginaceae*

Habitat: dry open slopes — May-June

This loosely branched perennial, 1½'-2' tall, is rather densely hairy. The basal leaves are long and slender with petioles equally as long. The leaves on the stem are much smaller and without petioles. The showy white flowers, which grow in a panicle, are about ¾" broad and have crested knob-like appendages at the throat of the petals.

Type locality: Dorleska Mine, Limedyke Lookout, Hobo Gulch

7. INSIDE-OUT FLOWER — BARBERRY FAMILY

Vancouvaria planipetala — *Berberidaceae*

Habitat: in forest shade at low elevations — June

This is a delicate plant with thread-like wiry stems 1'-1½' long. The leaflets of the compound leaves are thickish and roundish, about 1" in diameter, and bear a similarity in form to the maidenhair fern. The delicate white flowers have 6 reflexed petals and hang pendant in loose and open clusters of 25-50 flowers.

Type locality: Big Bar

8. INDIAN CARTWHEEL — PINK FAMILY

Silene hookeri ssp. *bolanderi* — *Caryophyllaceae*

Habitat: dry, rocky ground, open hillsides — May-June

The showy flowers of this plant are 1"-2" across and have 5 white or somewhat pinkish petals that stand out at right angles and are slashed into 4 narrow equal lobes. This subspecies differs from the species (see #169) in that these linear lobes of the petals are all the same length and nearly twice as long as those of the species. The stems are 3"-5" high with leaves that are grayish-green, narrowly oval, 1"-2" long and ½" wide.

Type locality: Musser Hill, Norwegian Meadows

9. STARWORT — PINK FAMILY

9. STARWORT | PINK FAMILY
Stellaria longipes | *Caryophyllaceae*
Habitat: wet meadows | July

This small plant has stems about 8" long and opposite leaves that are about 1" long. The flowers are usually but few and occasionally there may be only one. The petals are white, ¼" long, and nearly cleft to their base making the 5 petals appear to be as though there were 10.
Type locality: Big Flat

10. PEARLY EVERLASTING — SUNFLOWER FAMILY

10. PEARLY EVERLASTING | SUNFLOWER FAMILY
Anaphalis margaritacia | *Compositae*
Habitat: dry open places | August

There are usually several slender, erect, leafy and somewhat wooly stems 1'-2' high bearing numerous compact clusters of white flower heads about ¼" long. White, pointed, petal-like bracts give the blossoms their delightful pearly-white appearance. The leaves are narrow, 1"-4" long, and evenly distributed along the stem.
Type locality: Adams Lake Trail

11. BALLHEAD SANDWORT — PINK FAMILY

11. BALLHEAD SANDWORT | PINK FAMILY
Arenaria congesta | *Caryophyllaceae*
Habitat: dry rocky slopes | July

The flowering stem of this low herb, 4"-12" tall, is nearly leafless except for a very few small leaves. Most of the leaves are bunched at the base. They are needle-like and 1"-2½" long. There are numerous small white flowers ¼" long in a compact, head-like cluster at the tips of the stems. There may also be a smaller cluster on the stem an inch below it.
Type locality: Deadfall Lakes, LeRoy Mine Trail

12. NUTTALL'S SANDWORT — PINK FAMILY

12. NUTTALL'S SANDWORT | PINK FAMILY
Arenaria nuttallii var. *gregaria* | *Caryophyllaceae*
Habitat: loose, rocky and sandy slopes, high elevations | July

This is a low, mat-forming plant 3"-5" high with many sticky, rigid and somewhat awl-shaped leaves. The small white flowers each have 5 petals and 10 stamens and grow in loose clusters (cymes).
Type locality: Granite-Deer Creek Saddle, Sunrise Pass

13. FIELD CHICKWEED

Cerastium arvense
Habitat: moist banks

PINK FAMILY
Caryophyllaceae
July

The stems of this low herb are slender, erect, tufted, 3"-10" high, and usually sticky. The simple narrow or oblong leaves are ¾"-1¼" long. The white flowers have petals that are deeply cleft, making them somewhat star shaped. The flowers are about ¾" in diameter and few in number.
Type locality: Dorleska Mine, Josephine Lodge Road

14. YARROW

Achillea lanulosa
Habitat: meadows and open slopes

SUNFLOWER FAMILY
Compositae
July-August

This is an aromatic plant with simple stems 8"-30" tall. Its leaves are finely dissected, feathery in appearance, and 1½"-6" long. The flowers are in flat-topped clusters of numerous small white composite flowers. The individual outer petal-like ray flowers are only 1/8" long and surround a center area of tiny yellow disc flowers.
Type locality: Kidd Creek, Luella Lake, Leroy Mine Trail

15. WESTERN COLTSFOOT

Petasites palmatus
Habitat: shaded stream banks, lower elevations

SUNFLOWER FAMILY
Compositae
April

The large leaves of this plant are rounded, palmately lobed, and up to 16" broad. They rise from the rootstalk on stems about 16" long. Appearing in the spring before the leaves have developed are stout stems that are covered with leaf-like bracts. These bear a terminal cluster of dense heads of either mostly fertile pinkish ray flowers or mostly sterile disc flowers (see glossary).
Type locality: Big Bar, lower Trinity River

16. FRINGE-BRACT THISTLE

Cirsium callilepsis
Habitat: open woods

SUNFLOWER FAMILY
Compositae
June-August

This is a tall thistle having a simple stem 1'-3' high with spiny leaves 2"-12" long that are green above and paler and wooly beneath. The roundish flowers are creamy white, about 1" high, with fringe-tipped bracts beneath the flower head from which it gets its name.
Type locality: Norwegian Meadow, Doe Lake, Horse Haven Meadow

17. LACE POD   MUSTARD FAMILY
Thysanocarpus curvipes var. *elegans*   *Cruciferae*
Habitat: dry grassland, lower elevations   April

This is a weed-like plant about 18" high with erect stems bearing loose elongated racemes of minute whitish flowers. The fruit of this member of the mustard family is its most distinctive feature. It is a flattened pod, rounded in outline, with a marginal wing comprised of broad rays separated by perforated holes.
Type locality: Big Bar

18. PENNY CRESS   MUSTARD FAMILY
Thlaspi glaucum var. *hesperium*   *Cruciferae*
Habitat: dry slopes and meadows, higher elevations   June-August

This plant usually has several stems 4"-10" high growing from a common crown. They bear at their tips short dense racemes of creamy white flowers with petals less than ¼" long. As with all members of the mustard family this plant has characteristic 4 petals, 4 sepals, and 6 stamens.
Type locality: Yellow Rose Mine, Lake Anna

19. HILL MAN-ROOT, WILD CUCUMBER   GOURD FAMILY
Marah sp.   *Cucurbitaceae*
Habitat: usually dry slopes, lower elevations   April

This is an herb with trailing succulent stems that usually climb over nearby shrubs and trees. The leaves are rather large, thin, and somewhat ivy-like in shape. The flowers are small and whitish with a coralla that has 5-7 star-shaped lobes. The stamens and pistils are found in separate flowers. Those with the pistils are solitary and develop into large, dry, usually spiny fruits.
Type locality: Hyampom, French Creek

20. OX-EYE DAISY   SUNFLOWER FAMILY
Chrysanthemum leucanthemum   *Compositae*
Habitat: fields and roadsides   June-August

This pretty daisy looks very much like the Shasta daisy of domestic gardens. It has flower heads 1¼"-2" wide consisting of crisp white ray flowers and bright yellow disc flowers in a center area ½"-¾" in diameter. The stems are simple, 8"-24" long. Its leaves are coarsely toothed and widest at the tip. The lower leaves taper to a long petiole while the smaller leaves on the stem are almost sessile.
Type locality: Big Flat, Rush Creek, Highway 3

21. PINE-MAT MANZANITA   HEATH FAMILY
Arctostaphylos nevadensis   *Ericaceae*
Habitat: open slopes and woods   July

This is a low, spreading, intricately branched shrub from 4"-12" high.
Its spreading stems easily take root forming mat-like patches. The
leaves, about 1" long, are elliptic with a small point at the tip. Several
nodding, urn-shaped white flowers ¼" long are grouped together in a
compact erect cluster.
Type locality: Granite Lake Trail, Caribou Lakes Trail, Lake Eleanor

22. LABRADOR TEA   HEATH FAMILY
Ledum glandulosum var. *californicum*   *Ericaceae*
Habitat: banks of streams or lakes   July-August

This is a low, stiff shrub that is about 2' high with oblong, leathery, evergreen leaves that are crowded at the ends of the branches. The leaves
are from ½"-2½" long. There are numerous flowers in terminal rounded
compact clusters. The flowers have 5 spreading white petals ¼" long
and 10 rather conspicuous stamens.
Type locality: Conway Lake, Horseshoe Lake

23. BLACK LAUREL   HEATH FAMILY
Leucothoe davisiae   *Ericaceae*
Habitat: damp places, middle elevations   July

This is a shrubby plant 2'-5' high with terminal upright elongated racemes of pendulous white flowers. The blossoms are urn-shaped, about
¼" long. The stems bear crowded, oblong, evergreen leaves 1"-3" long.
Type locality: Canyon Creek

24. WHITE HEATHER   HEATH FAMILY
Cassiope mertensiana   *Ericaceae*
Habitat: damp rocky slopes, high elevations   July

This small shrub is about 1' high. Small scale-like leaves 1/8" long
clothe the branches. The numerous bell-like flowers grow in the axils of
the leaves. They are waxy-white, nodding, and about ¼" long.
Type locality: Grizzly Lake

25. FEW-FLOWERED BLEEDING HEART
Dicentra pauciflora
Habitat: damp gravelly slopes

BLEEDING HEART FAMILY
Fumariaceae
June-July

The stem of this unusual plant is 4"-5" high. The nodding flowers have 4 white or flesh colored petals. The two outer petals look like a flattened sack with a heart-shaped base and tips that are spreading and reflexed. The leaves are all basal and are finely divided into narrow segments.
Type locality: Horse Haven Meadow, Caribou Trail

26. WESTERN AZALEA
Rhododendron occidentale
Habitat: stream banks and moist places

HEATH FAMILY
Ericaceae
June-July

This loosely branching shrub, 3'-10' high, often grows in thickets. It has elliptical leaves 1"-4" long clustered at the ends of the branches. There are large clusters of fragrant and beautiful blossoms. The petals are white or pinkish and have a yellowish spot on the upper lobe. Five long, curving and conspicuous stamens protrude from the funnel-like tube of the flower.
Type locality: Lake Eleanor, Swift Creek Trail, Preacher Meadow

27. CATERPILLAR PLANT
Phacelia mutabilis
Habitat: light shade of rocky or gravelly slopes

WATERLEAF FAMILY
Hydrophyllaceae
June-July

The whitish flowers of this plant are in one-sided dense coiled (scorpioid) clusters which give it its common name. It is a hairy plant with pale green or grayish leaves crowded at the base and with smaller leaves scattered along the stem. The leaf blades, which are oval and come to a point at each end, have conspicuous parallel veins and occasionally a pair of small distinct lobes at the base.
Type locality: Big Flat, upper South Fork of the Salmon

28. DWARF HESPEROCHIRON
Hesperiochiron pumilus
Habitat: moist meadows

WATERLEAF FAMILY
Hydrophyllaceae
April-June

This is a stemless dwarf plant with oblong basal leaves about 2" long. There is one striking flower, saucer-shaped or flat, ¾" broad, whitish in color but with conspicuous pinkish veins and a yellow throat.
Type locality: Big Flat, Indian Creek

29. GROUND IRIS — IRIS FAMILY
Iris purdyi — *Iridaceae*
Habitat: open wooded slopes — May

The native iris are very difficult to identify as they hybridize easily. This one has flowering stems that are shorter than its long slender basal leaves. The flowers are most often white to pale cream with purplish or brownish veins. Distinguishing this species are many overlapping bract-like leaves which almost hide the flowering stem.
Type locality: Norwegian Meadow

30. SPANISH CLOVER — PEA FAMILY
Lotus purshianus var. *glauca* — *Leguminoseae*
Habitat: dry fields — June

This is a small delicate decumbent herb with silky foliage. The leaves usually have 3 leaflets 1" long. It is because of its 3 leaflets that the common name of clover has been attached to it although it is actually a lotus. Its tiny pea-like flower is whitish, tinged with rose, and is less than ¼" long.
Type locality: Norwegian Meadow

31. LONG-STALKED CLOVER — PEA FAMILY
Trifolium longipes — *Leguminoseae*
Habitat: damp places — June-July

The leaves of this clover generally have three narrow leaflets that are up to 2" long and ½" broad. Those near the base of the plant tend to be shorter and wider than the upper ones. Flower-stalks, 2"-6" long, stand erect well above the leaves giving it its common name. The individual flowers are cream to purplish in color and also stand erect in a dense head at the tip of the flower stalk.
Type locality: Upper South Fork of the Salmon

32. SISKIYOU LOCOWEED or BALLOON PLANT — PEA FAMILY
Astragalus whitneyi var. *siskiyouensis* — *Leguminoseae*
Habitat: open rocky slopes, high elevations — July

This is a low plant 10"-12" tall. Its stems have an uneven number of leaflets that are up to ¾" long and somewhat grayish in color. The whitish petals of the small 2-lipped flower quickly fade making its balloon-like fruiting pods its distinguishing characteristic. This inflated fruit is papery, translucent, and brightly mottled, 1½" long.
Type locality: Deadfall Lakes

33. BRIDE'S BONNET or CLINTONIA — LILY FAMILY
Clintonia uniflora — *Liliaceae*
Habitat: shaded woods — July

Sometimes carpeting the forest floor with its soft basal leaves 4"-6" long, this plant sends up a single lily-like flower on a stem shorter than the leaves. There are 6 white flower segments ¾"-1" long and ¼" wide.
Type locality: Granite Lake Trail, Canyon Creek

34. PUSSY EARS — LILY FAMILY
Calochortus tolmiei — *Liliaceae*
Habitat: dry rocky soil — April

The densely hairy petals of this member of the lily family are white or creamy, tinged with purplish-blue, and about ¾" long. The sepals beneath its 3 petals are about ½" long and often very blue. There is usually a single basal erect leaf 4"-6" long which is as long or longer than the flowering stem.
Type locality: Weaverville

35. FAIRY BELLS — LILY FAMILY
Disporum hookeri — *Liliaceae*
Habitat: shaded slopes and benches — May-June

The manner in which the branches and leaves of this plant grow in a horizontal plane is one of its distinguishing characteristics. The leaves are oblong, pointed at the tip and tightly clasp the stem. There are from 1 to 3 greenish-white pendulous bell-shaped flowers hanging beneath the leaves at the ends of the branches. These develop into scarlet berries late in the summer. (See also #36.)
Type locality: Boulder Creek

36. FAIRY BELLS (fruit)
Disporum hookeri
For description see #35.

37. FAWN LILY — LILY FAMILY
Erythronium californicum — *Liliaceae*
Habitat: open woods, lower elevations — April-May

This plant has 2 strongly mottled leaves 4"-6" long that emerge directly from the ground. One or more nodding flowers are at the end of a naked stem 4"-10" tall. The flower segments are white or cream with a pale yellow base, 1"-1½" long. The 6 stamens are noticeably large and white.
Type locality: Big French Creek, Musser Hill, Hyampom

38. BEAR GRASS — LILY FAMILY
Xerophyllum tenax — *Liliaceae*
Habitat: open dry slopes and woods — June

This is not a grass but a member of the lily family with an erect stem 2'-6' tall that is topped with a dense plume-like cluster of tiny white blossoms. At the base is a mound-like tuft of long, dry, rough-edged, slender "pampus grass"-like leaves. As with other members of the lily family the individual blossoms have 6 petal-like segments and 6 conspicuous stamens.
Type locality: Lake Eleanor Trail

39. TWISTED STALK — LILY FAMILY
Streptopus amplexifolius var. *denticulatus* — *Liliaceae*
Habitat: shaded stream banks — July

This plant is usually slightly larger than the fairy bells which it resembles, but with this the flowers are usually solitary in the axils of the leaves (see #35). The flowers hang on a thread-like stem which has a peculiar kink-like twist, accounting for its name. They are greenish-white, ½" long, with narrow spreading segments that curve back.
Type locality: Caribou Trail

40. CORN-LILY or FALSE HELLEBORE — LILY FAMILY
Veratrum californicum — *Liliaceae*
Habitat: wet meadows — July-August

The similarity in the growth habit of this plant to that of corn is the basis for the name which it has been given. It grows to a height of 3'-6' and has large parallel veined leaves up to a foot long. The stems are topped with a long, spreading, many-flowered dense cluster of small lily-like dull white flowers. Its six flower segments are up to ¾" long and have a green gland at their base.
Type locality: Big Flat, Bear Basin

41. GREENBRIER — LILY FAMILY
Smilax californica — *Liliaceae*
Habitat: in thickets along streambanks — May

This is a climbing or trailing plant with prickly stems up to 9' long. Its leaves have parallel veins and are more or less heart-shaped, 2"-4" long

and 2"-3" wide. Inconspicuous loose umbels of small greenish flowers hang on a slender stalk 1"-2" long from the axils of the leaves. Flowers with only pistils grow on one plant; flowers with only stamens grow on a different plant.
Type locality: Boulder Creek

42. CASCADE LILY — LILY FAMILY
Lilium washingtonium var. *purpurescens* — *Liliaceae*
Habitat: dry open granitic slopes — July

Growing 3'-6' tall, this Easter-type lily has leaves in whorls of 6-12 and flowers that are white which turn pink or wine color with age. In this variety of the species the flower segments overlap each other and are finely dotted with rose colored spots. With the species (*Lilium washingtonium*) the flower segments do not overlap and there are fewer spots. It is often seen growing in brushy areas. Both varieties are found in the Trinity mountains.
Type locality of variety illustrated: Swift Creek, Granite Peak Trail

43. STAR FLOWER — LILY FAMILY
Smilacina stellata — *Liliaceae*
Habitat: moist places — July

The dainty flowers of this plant grow in a loose elongated cluster at the end of a leafy stem 1'-2' high. They have 6 white petal-like segments and conspicuous excerted stamens. The leaves, which are up to 6" long and 1/6th as wide, clasp the stem and are usually folded along the midrib.
Type locality: Caribou Trail, Long Canyon

44. WESTERN SOLOMON'S SEAL — LILY FAMILY
Smilacina racemosa var. *amplexicaulis* — *Liliaceae*
Habitat: shaded woods — June

The unbranched leafy stems of this plant are 1'-3' long and bear an elongated terminal compound cluster of tiny white flowers. Long stamens extend beyond the petals and give the flower cluster a feathery aspect. Oblong pointed leaves 2"-3½" long clasp the stem and differentiate this variety from the regular species which has leaves with distinct petioles.
Type locality: Granite Lake Trail, Hobo Gulch Trail, Coffee Creek

45. COMMON TRILLIUM
Trillium chloropetalum
Habitat: wooded slopes

LILY FAMILY
Liliaceae
June

A whorl of 3 leaves distinguishes the trilliums. In this species the large leaves are up to 6" long and equally as broad. They are sometimes mottled. There are usually several stems 2"-20" high. The 3 narrow petals are greenish-white, 1½"-3½" long and sit directly on the whorl of leaves.
Type locality: Long Canyon, Grass Valley Creek

46. WESTERN TOLFIELDIA
Tolfieldia glutinosa ssp. *occidentalis*
Habitat: wet meadows and bogs

LILY FAMILY
Liliaceae
July-August

Solitary stems 1'-1½' tall bear at their tip a dense head-like cluster of small flowers. Each flower has 6 whitish, spreading, petal-like segments and 6 conspicuous broad stamens. The leaves, which are mostly basal, are narrow and grass-like.
Type locality: Black Basin, Yellow Rose Trail

47. WHITE-FLOWERED SCHOENOLIRION
Schoenolirion album
Habitat: wet meadows

LILY FAMILY
Liliaceae
June-July

This is a tall, slender, graceful plant 1'-3' tall with narrow, elongated basal leaves 1'-2' long. The flowers, which grow in an elongated spike-like cluster, are white with a dark central vein giving it a silvery aspect.
Type locality: Mumford Meadows, Norwegian Meadow, Kidd Creek Meadows.

48. WESTERN TRILLIUM
Trillium ovatum
Habitat: shaded woods

LILY FAMILY
Liliaceae
June-July

In contrast to the common trillium the flowers of this species stand above the whorl of three leaves on a short flower-stalk about 1" long. The showy white petals are more oval than those of the common trillium and turn rose color with age. The stems are from 5"-12" tall. (See #45.)
Type locality: Big French Creek

49. DEATH CAMAS

Zygadenus venenosus
Habitat: wet meadows

LILY FAMILY
Liliaceae
June

The slender stem of this plant is 10"-24" high and bears a loose raceme of whitish flowers. There is a conspicuous yellow gland at the base of each petal-like segment. The leaves are all basal. They are narrow, usually folded, and half as long as the flower stalk. All parts of the plant are highly toxic.
Type locality: Norwegian Meadow, Lake Eleanor

50. BOG REIN-ORCHID

Habenaria dilatata var. *leucostachys*
Habitat: wet places

ORCHID FAMILY
Orchidaceae
June-July

The leafy stem of this plant is 1'-3' tall and has a terminal spike of orchid-like white flowers having a prominent spur that is ½"-¾" long. The leaves are narrow, pointed, and up to 8" long.
Type locality: Lake Eleanor, Horse Haven Meadows, Stuarts Fork

51. SLENDER PHLOX

Microsteris gracilis ssp. *humilis*
Habitat: dry slopes

PHLOX FAMILY
Polemoneaceae
June

This is an inconspicuous annual about 4" high with simple leaves that are crowded with hoary fine hairs. The small flowers, growing in a dense and sticky head, are tubular with 5 spreading flat lobes less than 1/8" long. Although they are usually white, they often take on a pinkish or lavender tinge.
Type locality: Horse Haven Meadows

52. NUTTALL'S LINANTHUS

Linanthus nuttallii
Habitat: dry open slopes

PHLOX FAMILY
Polemoneaceae
July-August

This is a thickly branched and leafy perennial 6"-10" tall. The leaves are opposite and divided into narrow segments about ½" long. The flowers, which grow in crowded heads, are funnel-like, white with a yellowish tube, and about ½" long.
Type locality: Foster Lake, Sunrise Pass Trail, Dorleska Mine

53. PHANTOM ORCHID — ORCHID FAMILY
Cephalanthera austinae — *Orchidaceae*
Habitat: damp woods, middle elevations — June

There are no green leaves on this ghostly white plant, only a few sheathing scales. It grows to a height of 10"-20" and bears a terminal cluster of waxy white flowers. They have a spot of yellow in the throat and are about ½" long. This is a rare saprophyte.
Type locality: Lion Lake Trail, Rancheria Trail

54. CALIFORNIA LADY SLIPPER — ORCHID FAMILY
Cypripedium californicum — *Orchidaceae*
Habitat: wet places in open woods — June

The inflated lower lip of this orchid looks more like a baby's bootie than a lady's slipper but it distinguishes this plant from its associates. The inflated sac-like lower petal is usually white. The other petals and sepals are a greenish-yellow. The flowers are about 1¼" broad and grow along the upper stem in the axils of the leaf-like bracts. The stems can be as much as 2' tall and bear 3-10 flowers.
Type locality: Swift Creek

55. COMPOSITE BUCKWHEAT — BUCKWHEAT FAMILY
Eriogonum compositum — *Polygonaceae*
Habitat: dry rocky slopes — July

The stout leafless stems of this wild buckwheat are from ½'-1½' long. The leaves, which are all basal, are green or reddish-green above and white-wooly beneath. They are 1"-4" long with a petiole equally as long. The compact head-like umbels of tiny cream colored flowers are larger and more conspicuous than those of other buckwheats in this area.
Type locality: Diamond Lake, Deer Lake

56. NEEDLE-LEAVED NAVARRETIA — PHLOX FAMILY
Navarretia intertexta — *Polemoniaceae*
Habitat: open meadows — July

This is a dwarf annual about 2"-4" high with crowded needle-like leaves ½"-¾" long. Crowded in a dense head are several tubular, white to pale lavender or blue flowers. The 5 lobes of the flower are broad and about ¼" long.
Type locality: Packer Meadow

57. NEVADA LEWISIA — PURSLANE FAMILY

Lewisia nevadensis — *Portulacaceae*

Habitat: damp meadows — June

This is a dwarf plant with thick, succulent, basal leaves up to 2½" long, exceeding in length the leafless flower-stalk. There may be one or more stems ½"-4" long, each bearing a single showy white, or sometimes pinkish, flower having from 5-9 petals about ½" long.
Type locality: Swift Creek, Preacher Meadow, Packer Meadow

58. KNOTWEED — BUCKWHEAT FAMILY

Polygonum bistortoides — *Polygonaceae*

Habitat: wet meadows — June-August

The simple, erect, slender, grass-like stems of this plant are 1'-2' tall with long, narrow and smooth leaves that are mostly basal, 4"-5" long. The tiny white flowers are in a dense terminal spike from ½"-1½" long. Do not confuse this with the naked buckwheat (see #59) or the western tolfieldia (see #46).
Type locality: Yellow Rose Trail, Kidd Creek

59. NAKED STEM BUCKWHEAT — BUCKWHEAT FAMILY

Eriogonum latifolium ssp. *nudum* — *Polygonaceae*

Habitat: dry rocky slopes — July-August

Slender, sparingly branched, naked stems 1'-3' tall distinguish this buckwheat. The leaves are basal, somewhat oval, green above and white wooly beneath, 1"-2" long. The compact heads of tiny flowers at the ends of the stems are white or cream, tinged with rose or yellow.
Type locality: Yellow Rose Mine, Long Canyon, Swift Creek

60. THREE-LEAVED LEWISIA — PURSLANE FAMILY

Lewisia triphylla — *Portulacaceae*

Habitat: damp places — July

This small Lewisia does not have basal leaves as does the Nevada Lewisia and the flowers are smaller (see #57). Instead, there are 3 to 5 narrow succulent leaves borne on the stem. The flowers may have from 5 to 10 white or pinkish petals ¼" long.
Type locality: Horse Haven Meadow, Willow Creek Basin

61. FROSTED MINER'S LETTUCE   PURSLANE FAMILY
Montia perfoliata forma *glauca*   *Portulacaceae*
Habitat: rocky places in ponderosa pine forests   June

This is one of the variable forms of the miner's lettuce. (See #62 and #203.) This form is distinguished by the whitish bloom on its foliage.
Type locality: Long Canyon Trail

62. MINER'S LETTUCE   PURSLANE FAMILY
Montia perfoliata   *Portulacaceae*
Habitat: damp places   April

This is a lush plant deserving of its name. The stems are somewhat erect and from 4"-12" tall. At the upper end of the stem two opposite leaves are joined to form a disc beneath a loose group of small white flowers that have petals about ¼" long. The other leaves are basal. Variations in the leaves account for several of the varieties that have been identified. In this case the basal leaves have long petioles and a blade that is somewhat diamond shaped.
Type locality: Indian Creek

63. SIBERIAN MONTIA   PURSLANE FAMILY
Montia sibirica   *Portulacaceae*
Habitat: damp places   May-June

This Montia has two distinct leaves on the stem. They are not joined into a disc as with our other Montia (see miner's lettuce #62). There are several broadly oval basal leaves 1"-2" long with petioles that are twice as long. The flowers are in a loose cluster and have white petals with pink veins. These petals are about ¼" long and have a small notch in the tip.
Type locality: Battle Creek, Boulder Creek

64. ONE-SIDED WINTERGREEN   WINTERGREEN FAMILY
Pyrola secunda   *Pyrolaceae*
Habitat: dry shaded woods   July

The white to greenish bell-like flowers of this small plant all turn to one side of a simple stem 4"-7" tall. The flowers are about 3/8" long and have a characteristic protruding style. The leaves are basal, oval, and have somewhat scalloped or toothed margins.
Type locality: Kidd Creek Trail

65. INDIAN PIPE — WINTERGREEN FAMILY
Monotropa uniflora — *Pyrolaceae*
Habitat: shade of damp woods — July

This is a waxy white saprophyte with no green leaves. It has a solitary nodding flower that bears a resemblance to an Indian pipe. There is usually a group of several stems from 4"-12" long. As the plant dries the waxy color blackens. Rare.
Type locality: Boulder Creek

66. WHITE-VEINED SHINLEAF — WINTERGREEN FAMILY
Pyrola picta — *Pyrolaceae*
Habitat: humus of dry forests — June-July

The leaves of this plant are its most distinguishing characteristic. They are all basal, 1"-3" long, and are dark green with white vein-like markings. The flowers are evenly spaced along the upper end of a 4"-10" flower stalk. The cream to greenish, concave waxy petals are cup-shaped, nodding, and about ¼" long. A subspecies, *Pyrola picta ssp. dentata,* is very similar except that the leaves do not have the white markings and are usually smaller. It has been observed along the Swift Creek trail.
Type locality: Boulder Creek, Deer Creek

67. BUCKBRUSH — BUCKTHORN FAMILY
Ceanothus cuneatus — *Rhamnaceae*
Habitat: dry gravelly ground, lower elevations — May

This is a much-branched rigid shrub with gray bark. It usually forms dense thickets. The gray-green evergreen leaves are thick and wedge-shaped, ¼"-½" long. Small showy clusters of tiny white flowers grow at the end of spur-like branchlets. The individual flower stems in these flower clusters come from a common point (an umbel). This is in contrast to the whitethorn in which the flower clusters are about the same size but the individual stems do not originate at one point (see #70).
Type locality: Weaverville

68. DRUMMOND'S ANEMONE — BUTTERCUP FAMILY
Anemone drummondii — *Ranunculaceae*
Habitat: talus or gravelly slopes, higher elevations — July

This plant usually has several stems up to 1' high. The leaves are finely dissected and covered with soft hairs. The solitary flower at the end of the stem has petal-like sepals ⅓"-¾" long that are white and often tinged with blue on the underside.
Type locality: Long Canyon

69. WESTERN PASQUE FLOWER   BUTTERCUP FAMILY
or MOUNTAIN ANEMONE   *Ranunculaceae*
Anemone occidentalis   July-August
Habitat: open slopes, higher elevations

This plant emerges behind receding snow banks. There are several stems about 1' high. Each bears a single white flower that has 5 or 6 petal-like white sepals up to 1¼" long. True petals are lacking. There are numerous stamens and pistils. The showy flowers are fully formed before the finely dissected leaves have completely developed. Following flowering the fruits form large and conspicuous globose heads of plumose seeds.
Type locality: Deer Lake, Long Canyon, Caribou Lake

70. MOUNTAIN WHITETHORN   BUCKTHORN FAMILY
Ceanothus cordulatus   *Rhamnaceae*
Habitat: dry slopes   June

This is a low, thorny, much branched shrub with rigid, crooked, light gray branches. The oval leaves are ½"-¾" long and have 3 prominent veins. The tiny white flowers are in small, dense clusters about 1" across in which the stems of the individual flowers do not originate at a common point as with the buckbrush (see #67).
Type locality: Long Canyon, Tule Creek Road

71. WOOD ANEMONE   BUTTERCUP FAMILY
Anemone deltoidea   *Ranunculaceae*
Habitat: shaded woods   June-July

This delicate slender plant, 3"-6" tall, has a whorl of 3 broad leaves 1"-2" long just above the middle of the stem. At the tip of the stem is a single flower with 5 showy white sepals ½" long. There are no real petals. Especially noticeable are the numerous white stamens.
Type locality: Kidd Creek, Backbone Creek, Yellow Rose Mine Trail

72. MARSH MARIGOLD   BUTTERCUP FAMILY
Caltha howellii   *Ranunculaceae*
Habitat: marshy or boggy places   July

This is a fleshy plant with simple, large, roundish, mostly basal leaves 1½"-4" wide. The flowers are single at the ends of naked stems 12" long. There are no petals but the showy white oblong sepals are about 5/8" long and look like petals. There are numerous conspicuous yellow stamens.
Type locality: Kidd Creek, Long Canyon, Ward Lake

73. SNOWBRUSH   BUCKTHORN FAMILY
Ceanothus velutinus   *Rhamnaceae*
Habitat: open wooded slopes   June-July

This is an evergreen shrub with shiny oval leaves 1"-2½" long that have 3 prominent veins and are dark green and gummy above and paler beneath. The dense clusters of tiny white flowers are 1"-2" long. The shrub grows to a height of 5'-6' and has a strong aromatic odor.
Type locality: Yellow Rose Mine Trail, Stuarts Fork Trail, Weaver Bally

74. COFFEEBERRY   BUCKTHORN FAMILY
Rhamnus californica ssp. *occidentallis*   *Rhamnaceae*
Habitat: dry slopes   June

This rounded shrub growing to a height of 5' has elliptical leaves 1½"-2½" long. They have prominent parallel veins and are green above and yellowish beneath. The flowers, which are very small and inconspicuous, have creamy white, somewhat star-shaped petals 1/8" long.
Type locality: Lake Eleanor

75. NINE-BARK   ROSE FAMILY
Physocarpus capitatus   *Rosaceae*
Habitat: stream-banks   July

This is an erect or straggly shrub up to 5' high with leaves that are palmately lobed in the manner of the vine maple. The leaves are irregularly toothed and from 1¼"-2¾" long. The flowers are rounded clusters (corymbs) of small flowers that have 5 spreading round white petals 1/8" long and numerous stamens. Its name is derived from its shreddy bark which appears to have "nine" layers.
Type locality: Granite Lake Trail

76. WOOD STRAWBERRY   ROSE FAMILY
Fragaria californica   *Rosaceae*
Habitat: open woods   June

This is a low growing, creeping plant that spreads by runners. The leaves have 3 rounded, coarsely toothed leaflets with a petiole 1½"-5" long. There are usually 2 flowers ¾" broad that have 5 white petals and numerous stamens.
Type locality: Boulder Creek

77. THIMBLEBERRY ROSE FAMILY
Rubus parviflorus *Rosaceae*
Habitat: open woods and canyons June-August

This is a low, branching, woody plant without prickles. The large and conspicuous leaves are 4"-6" wide and palmately divided into 5 lobes. It has a single showy blossom 1"-2" across which is similar in appearance to the flower of the wood strawberry (see #76).
Type locality: Lion Lake Trail

78. DUSKY HORKELIA ROSE FAMILY
Horkelia fusca ssp. *parviflora* *Rosaceae*
Habitat: dry flats and meadows July-August

This "weedy" plant has leaves which are mostly basal and divided into several pairs of wedge-shaped leaflets that are in turn incised into small lobes. The flowers are in compact clusters at the ends of slender, nearly leafless stems 1'-1½' tall. There are 5 widely spaced, wedge-shaped, white to pinkish petals 1/8" long and 10 very short stamens.
Type locality: Horse Haven Meadows

79. SERVICEBERRY ROSE FAMILY
Amelanchier alnifolia *Rosaceae*
Habitat: open slopes June

This loosely branching shrub grows to be about 6' tall. It has oval leaves 1"-2" long that have the distinguishing feature of being toothed along the margins of only the upper half of the leaf. The flowers have 5 narrow white petals ½" long that are slightly twisted. This gives them an irregular and straggly appearance. The fruit is blue-black, about ¼" in diameter, and is edible.
Type locality: Big Flat, Canyon Creek, Stuarts Fork

80. OCEAN SPRAY ROSE FAMILY
Holodiscus microphyllus *Rosaceae*
Habitat: dry slopes and ridges August

This is a brushy shrub about 4' high. Its distinctive leaves, about 1" long, are wider and toothed at the top and narrower and not toothed at the base. Its plume-like clusters of foam-like flowers are befitting its name. Its unopened buds are perfect spheres.
Type locality: Dorleska Trail, East Weaver Lake

81. GRAY'S BEDSTRAW
Galium grayanum ssp. *glabrescens*
Habitat: dry rocky slopes, higher elevations

MADDER FAMILY
Rubiaceae
July

This is a small plant with several stout stems 6" tall. The leaves, in whorls of 4, are broad, about 1/4"-3/8" long, and have a sharp rigid point at the tip. The flowers are small with 4 greenish-white petals that are conspicuously covered with long hairs.
Type locality: Gulick Creek Drainage, Deadfall Lake Trail

82. SWEET BEDSTRAW
Galium triflorum
Habitat: moist shaded canyons

MADDER FAMILY
Rubiaceae
June

This fragile plant has low, slender, trailing stems that are 4-angled and have a sandpapery feeling to the touch. There are 6 slender leaves in whorls that are widely spaced along the stem. The flowers are usually in groups of 3 on slender stems in the axils of the leaves. Its 4 greenish-white petals are joined together at the base like a tiny cross.
Type locality: Yellow Rose Mine Trail

83. WILD CURRANT
Ribes viscosissimum
Habitat: shaded woods

SAXIFRAGE FAMILY
Saxifragaceae
June

This small shrub is 2'-3' tall with roundish, palmately lobed leaves that have a heart-shaped base. Several flowers are borne in elongated racemes. They are sticky, about ½" long, with 5 spreading outer greenish to pinkish sepals and 5 smaller white petals that stand erect in the center. Currants are generally similar to gooseberries but do not have spines.
Type locality: Lion Lake Trail, Caribou Trail

84. MOUNTAIN BOYKINIA
Boykinia major
Habitat: damp areas along streams

SAXIFRAGE FAMILY
Saxifragaceae
July

This is a stout plant 2'-3' high with large leaves 4"-8" broad that are roundish in outline, clefted, and coarsely toothed. The flowers are in dense flattish clusters. Five white petals about ¼" long alternate with 5 smaller, slender, triangular sepals. Yellow nectar glands in the center make the flower attractive to insects.
Type locality: Boulder Creek Falls, Stuarts Fork Trail

119

85. GRASS-OF-PARNASSUS
Parnassia palustris var. *californica*
Habitat: marshy areas and wet places

SAXIFRAGE FAMILY
Saxifragaceae
August

Usually found growing in small groups, this plant has a simple stem 1'-1½' tall. It bears one greenish-white flower that has 5 conspicuously veined petals about ½" long. The leaves are basal, egg-shaped, 1"-1½" long, and taper to a petiole equally as long.
Type locality: Swift Creek Trail, Kidd Creek

86. ALUM ROOT
Heuchera micrantha
Habitat: rocky cliffs

SAXIFRAGE FAMILY
Saxifragaceae
June-July

This plant has a slender flower stalk 1'-2' tall rising from a rosette of roundish and lobed leaves. Each stalk bears a delicate, elongated, compound cluster (panicle) of tiny white flowers.
Type locality: Hobo Gulch Road, Long Canyon

87. INDIAN RHUBARB
Peltiphyllum peltatum
Habitat: borders of streams

SAXIFRAGE FAMILY
Saxifragaceae
June-July

The large umbrella-like leaves are 1'-2' across and attached in the middle to a long stalk that may reach 4' in length. The large saucer-shaped leaves are the most conspicuous part of the plant. A naked flower-stalk 10"-40" long bearing a loose, rounded cluster of pink or white flowers emerges before the leaves. The flowers have 5 rounded petals ¼" long, 10 conspicuous awl-shaped stamens, and pistils that become reddish with age.
Type locality: Alpine Lake Trail, Boulder Creek Trail

88. WOODLAND STAR
Lithophragma parviflora
Habitat: open woods

SAXIFRAGE FAMILY
Saxifragaceae
April-July

The simple slender flowering stems of this delicate plant are 1'-1½' tall and bear a few to several white to pinkish flowers. The deeply divided petals of this species give them a star-like appearance. The leaves are basal, roundish in outline, and lobed. There is a similar species known as the hill-star (*Lithophragma heterophylla*) growing at middle elevations which has basal leaves that are only shallowly lobed and white flowers with a squared off base whose petals are but shallowly cleft.
Type locality, Woodland Star: Indian Creek
Type locality, Hill Star: Horse Haven Trail, Willow Creek Basin

89. LEAFY LOUSEWORT
Pedicularis racemosa
Habitat: dry shaded slopes

FIGWORT FAMILY
Scrophulareaceae
August

This plant usually has several slender stems 1'-1½' long and narrow pointed leaves 1"-2" long that have finely toothed margins. The flowers are whitish to purple-tinged and grow in the axils of leafy bracts. The upper lip of the corolla is compressed and curved into a tapering arched beak; the lower lip has 3 lobes.
Type locality: Kidd Creek Trail

90. SNOWDROP BUSH
Styrax officinalis var. *californica*
Habitat: dry slopes, lower elevations

STORAX FAMILY
Styracaceae
April

This deciduous shrub has simple leaves 1"-3½" long. White flowers bearing a similarity to orange blossoms grow on short stems in small clusters at the ends of its many branches. There are usually 6 petals about ½" long united at the base and twice as many stamens as there are petal lobes.
Type locality: Lewiston Turnpike

91. YERBA DE SELVA
Whipplea modesta
Habitat: moist or shaded slopes, lower elevations

SAXIFRAGE FAMILY
Saxifragaceae
June

This is a low, slender, trailing, slightly woody plant with opposite leaves that are oval, about 1" long and usually with sparsely toothed margins. Crowded at the ends of the simple erect stems are 4-9 tiny flowers with both the sepals and petals white in color.
Type locality: Eagle Creek Ranch (Big Bar)

92. YAMPAH
Perideridia parishii
Habitat: wet or dry meadows

PARSLEY FAMILY
Umbelliferae
July-August

This is a much smaller member of the parsley family than the other species described in this section. The somewhat flat-topped lacy clusters of minute flowers are at the end of flower-stalks 1'-2' tall. The leaves are up to 6" long and are usually divided into 2 or 3 narrow, grass-like segments.
Type locality: Horse Haven Meadows

93. CALIFORNIA LOVAGE · PARSLEY FAMILY

Ligusticum californicum — *Umbelliferae*

Habitat: open meadows and slopes — August

This plant resembles the angelica but it is not as large. The leaves are more lace-like and are doubly or triply cleft into narrow lobes (see #94). It grows to a height of 2'-3'. The flower-stalks are up to 12" long and bear terminal compound umbels of tiny white flowers.
Type locality: Kidd Creek Meadows, Mumford Meadows

94. ANGELICA · PARSLEY FAMILY

Angelica arguta — *Umbelliferae*

Habitat: dry slopes and meadows — July

This stout plant, up to 4' tall, is sometimes confused with the cow-parsnip but the flower heads of the angelica are spherical, not flat-topped as with the cow-parsnip (see #95) and there are also noticeable differences in the leaves. The leaves of the angelica are nearly 8" long and are twice divided. The ultimate leaflets are long-oval in outline and up to 3" long and 1" wide.
Type locality: Deer Creek Meadows, Summit Lake, Big Flat

95. COW-PARSNIP · PARSLEY FAMILY

Heracleum lanatum — *Umbelliferae*

Habitat: damp meadows — July

This immense plant with stout hollow stems 4'-9' tall has huge, broad, mostly basal leaves that are divided into 3 very large, irregularly tooth-ed leaflets each of which may be as much as 8"-12" long. The upper stem supports very large compound umbels of tiny white flowers. Its seeds are flattened, oval, somewhat heart-shaped, and about $\frac{1}{3}$" long. There are 4 dark lines alternating with 3 fine ribs on each of the flat-tened sides of the seeds helping to identify the plant late in the season.
Type locality: Gulick Creek, Horse Haven Meadows

96. MACLOSKEY'S VIOLET · VIOLET FAMILY

Viola macloskeyi — *Violaceae*

Habitat: wet meadows — June-July

This violet has rounded and kidney-shaped leaves with slender petioles that emerge from nodes on the creeping stolons. The flowers stand taller than the leaves and have white petals about 3/8" long with the 3 lower petals having purple veins.
Type locality: Swift Creek, Long Canyon, Mavis Lake

97. GOLDEN BRODIAEA
Brodiaea lutea var. *analina*
Habitat: grassy slopes in open woods

AMARYLLIS FAMILY
Amaryllidaceae
May

The dull yellow flowers of this brodiaea have a dark brownish mid-vein on the outside of each segment. The segments spread in a funnel-like manner and are between ½" and ¾" long. There are usually 4-7 flowers growing in a loose and open umbel on a slender stem 8" or more long. The anthers of the stamens are sometimes blue.
Type locality: Preacher Meadow, Buckhorn Mountain

98. ORANGE HONEYSUCKLE
Lonicera ciliosa
Habitat: dry slopes, lower elevations

HONEYSUCKLE FAMILY
Caprifoliaceae
June

This is a trailing shrub, 2'-18' long, with oval leaves that are 1½"-3½" long and up to 2" wide. The uppermost leaves are often joined so as to appear to be one leaf enclosing the stem. The flowers are trumpet-shaped, slightly 2-lipped, ¾"-1¼" long, yellow to reddish orange in color. They grow in a single terminal whorl at the ends of the branches.
Type locality: Stony Creek

99. ORANGE FLOWERED AGOSERIS
Agoseris aurantiaca
Habitat: moist meadows, high elevations

SUNFLOWER FAMILY
Compositae
July

Single flowers grow on stems 4"-20" tall and are burnt orange in color turning purple with age. The long narrow leaves are mostly basal, 2"-8" long, and variously toothed much like those of a dandelion.
Type locality: Horse Haven Meadows

100. MOUNTAIN ARNICA
Arnica latifolia
Habitat: moist rocks and stream-banks

SUNFLOWER FAMILY
Compositae
July

This plant has stems 4"-18" tall that usually bear 3 pairs of opposite leaves 1½"-4" long. They are elliptic, pointed and irregularly toothed along the margins. The flower heads have 8-12 clear yellow ray flowers ½"-1" long. There may be more than one head on a stem.
Type locality: Upper South Fork of the Salmon

101. RABBITBRUSH
Chrysothamnus nauseosus var. *occidentalis*
Habitat: open dry slopes

SUNFLOWER FAMILY
Compositae
September

This low woody shrub, 1'-3' high, has many stems bearing very narrow grayish-green leaves about 1/8" wide and from ¾"-2" long. When in bloom the entire shrub is covered with a mass of yellow flowers. The individual flowers of each composite head are all disc flowers and less than ½" long.
Type locality: Bonanza King Mountain

102. WOOLY SUNFLOWER
Eriophyllum lanatum var. *lanceolatum*
Habitat: dry locations

SUNFLOWER FAMILY
Compositae
June

This is a very diverse species with many varieties having been identified. The leaves are generally lobed to one degree or another, white-wooly in appearance, and from ½"-3" long. The plant grows to a height of 1'-2'. The flowers are usually solitary on long flower-stalks. Both disc and ray flowers are a bright yellow and form a head 1"-1½" broad.
Type locality: Canyon Creek, Coffee Creek, Battle Creek

103. HOUNDSTONGUE HAWKWEED
Hieracium cynoglossoides var. *nudicaule*
Habitat: open woods

SUNFLOWER FAMILY
Compositae
July-August

This is a weed-like plant with nearly naked slender stems about 12" high. The leaves are slender and basal, 4" or more long, and very hairy. The bright yellow flower heads have only ray flowers which are about ⅓" long and grow in open and sparse clusters at the ends of the sparsely branched stems.
Type locality: Horse Haven Meadows, Kidd Creek

104. ROCK DAISY
Erigeron petrophilus
Habitat: open and rocky slopes

SUNFLOWER FAMILY
Compositae
August

This plant usually has several erect leafy stems 4"-12" tall that bear numerous narrowly-oval, somewhat sticky leaves ½"-¾" long. This is a member of the sunflower family in which there are no petal-like ray flowers but yellow disc flowers only. Each stem bears 1-4 flower heads about ⅓" in diameter.
Type locality: Yellow Rose Mine

105. CALIFORNIA LITTLE SUNFLOWER SUNFLOWER FAMILY
Helianthella californica   *Compositae*
Habitat: grassy slopes and openings in woods   May

The flower heads of this species are borne singly on leafless stems 1'-2'
long. The leaves, which are mostly basal, are narrow and tapering, 5"-
10" long. The center of small yellow disc flowers is about ¾" in diameter. This is surrounded by approximately 11 petal-like ray flowers.
Type locality: Musser Hill

106. BIGELOW SNEEZEWEED   SUNFLOWER FAMILY
Helenium bigelovii   *Compositae*
Habitat: moist meadows and along streams   July-August

The center flowers of most members of the sunflower family are called
disc or tubular flowers and the outer petal-like flowers are ray or strap
flowers. In this case the disc flowers are golden-brown and form a dome.
The ray flowers are yellow or bronze and tend to droop downward. They
are widest at the tip and are about ½"-¾" long. The stems, which are
few and from 1'-1½' tall, bear but a few long, narrow leaves.
Type locality: Horse Haven Meadows, Swift Creek, Lake Eleanor

107. COMMON MADIA   SUNFLOWER FAMILY
Madia elegans   *Compositae*
Habitat: dry hillsides, dry meadows   June

This is a hairy or sticky plant 2'-3' tall with narrow leaves. The lower
leaves are 3"-5" long and the upper leaves much shorter. The upper half
of the stem is much branched and bears yellow flower heads from 1"-2"
across. The tips of the outer ray flowers are incised into 3 lobes. The
stamens of the center disc flowers are often tipped with black. These
flowers close during the bright light of midday.
Type locality: Norwegian Meadow

108. GUM PLANT   SUNFLOWER FAMILY
Grindelia camporum   *Compositae*
Habitat: dry soils, lower elevations   June

Gumweeds are so named because of the resin they exude, especially at
the flower head which is quite sticky. There are several woody stems
about 2' high with sharply toothed leaves 1"-3" long. The yellow flower
heads are 1"-1½" across and are subtended by bracts whose narrow
tips bend sharply down.
Type locality: Weaverville

109. CALIFORNIA CONE-FLOWER   SUNFLOWER FAMILY
Rudbeckia californica   *Compositae*
Habitat: moist meadows   June-July

This member of the sunflower family grows to be nearly 6' tall with un-branched but leafy stems. The leaves are oval or elliptic and up to 10" long. A single showy flower is borne on a long smooth flower stalk. The center disc portion is raised into a cone an inch or more high. The outer petal-like ray flowers are 1"-2½" long and number from 8 to 21.
Type locality: Lake Eleanor, Scott Mountain

110. ARROWLEAF SENECIO   SUNFLOWER FAMILY
Senecio triangularis   *Compositae*
Habitat: moist slopes at higher elevations   July-August

This is a vigorous plant commonly 3' tall. The triangular or arrowhead shape of the leaves distinguishes this plant. The leaves vary in length from 1½"-5" long and are usually sharply toothed and well distributed along the stem. Flower heads are numerous in a relatively flat-topped cluster. There are usually about 8 ray flowers ⅓"-½" long in each composite head.
Type locality: Mumford Meadows, Swift Creek, Gulick Creek, South Fork Mountain

111. SINGLE-STEMMED BUTTERWEED   SUNFLOWER FAMILY
Senecio integerrimus var. *major*   *Compositae*
Habitat: partial shade of forest slopes   June-July

This plant, with its single stem, is 1'-1½' tall. Its leaves are mostly basal although there are some small leaves borne alternately on the stem. The plant is more or less covered with cobwebby hairs. A relatively few heads of yellow flowers make up a somewhat flat-topped cluster. Each head has 5 to 7 ray flowers ½" long as well as disc flowers of the same length.
Type locality: LeRoy Mine area

112. MULE-EARS   SUNFLOWER FAMILY
Wyethia angustifolia   *Compositae*
Habitat: open meadows   May-June

The large pointed leaves, bearing a similarity to a mule's ear, distin-guish this plant. They are about 3" wide, 7"-15" long, and crowded

at the base of the plant. The flower heads are usually single at the end of stems 1'-2' long. Their showy heads are about 2"-3" across and have from 10-17 petal-like ray flowers, bright yellow in color.
Type locality: Norwegian Meadow, East Fork Trinity River

113. ALPINE GOLDENROD   SUNFLOWER FAMILY
Solidago multiradiata   *Compositae*
Habitat: open rocky places, high elevations   August

This goldenrod is less than 1½' tall. It has lance-shaped leaves which decrease in size from 4" long near the base to about 1" long at the upper end of the stem. The flower heads form a rather loose flat-topped cluster. In contrast to the meadow goldenrod, the ray flowers greatly exceed the disc flowers in length (see #114).
Type locality: Dorleska Mine

114. MEADOW GOLDENROD   SUNFLOWER FAMILY
Solidago canadensis ssp. *elongata*   *Compositae*
Habitat: meadows and stream banks   July-September

The simple erect leafy stems of this goldenrod are 2'-3' tall. The numerous leaves which crowd the stem are rather uniform in size, taper to a point at each end, and about ½"-2" long. The flower heads have very short and narrow ray flowers that barely exceed the disc flowers in length. They are numerous and congested into an elongated cluster 2"-8" long.
Type locality: Horse Haven Meadows, Horseshoe Lake

115. RAILLARDELLA   SUNFLOWER FAMILY
Raillardella pringlei   *Compositae*
Habitat: wet places   August

This is a rare species with very limited distribution. The flower is borne singly on stems 12"-16" long. The narrow leaves are mostly basal and up to 4" long. There are 6-10 orange petal-like ray flowers. The rays are broad and incised into 3 lobes. The stem just below the flower head is quite sticky.
Type locality: Mumford Meadows, Landers Lake

116. HAWKSBEARD
Crepis pleurocarpa
Habitat: dry rocky slopes and meadows

SUNFLOWER FAMILY
Compositae
June-August

This is a weed-like plant bearing a few to several flowers in an open and loose cluster on a nearly naked stem 10"-16" high. The mostly basal leaves are about 10" long and deeply incised. Since this is a member of the sunflower family each flower head is a composite of a few to many individual flowers. In this case there are but 5 individual flowers each having a narrow petal-like strap about ¾" long.
Type locality: Dorleska Mine, Luella Lake Trail

117. YELLOW SALSIFY
Tragopogon dubius
Habitat: waste places

SUNFLOWER FAMILY
Compositae
June-July

This is a weed-like plant sometimes known as the goat dandelion because of the long bracts that are much longer than the flower. The heads of pale lemon-yellow flowers are solitary and when in fruit form conspicuous spheres about 3" in diameter containing over 100 plumose seeds. This is a dandelion-type plant having only ray flowers. There is a closely related species with purple flowers.
Type locality: Trinity Center, Weaverville

118. SIERRA WALLFLOWER
Erysimum perenne
Habitat: dry slopes, higher elevations

MUSTARD FAMILY
Cruciferae
August

This wallflower is smaller than the western wallflower of lower elevations (see #120). It usually has a single stem about 1' tall bearing narrow, widely spaced leaves that are 1"-2" long. The flowers, which are about ½" long, are a lighter yellow and usually smaller than those of the western wallflower.
Type locality: Kidd Creek Basin

119. DYER WOAD
Isastis tinctoria
Habitat: roadsides and waste places

MUSTARD FAMILY
Cruciferae
June

This is an established weed with branched stems 2'-3' tall. The basal oblong leaves are 4" long. Those on the stem are much smaller. The branching flower clusters bear numerous small groups of tiny yellow

flowers 1/8" long. The fruit when mature is distinctive. It is flat, some-what pear-shaped, dark purple in color, ½" long and ¼" wide, and hangs pendulous on a slender stem.
Type locality: Coffee Creek

120. WESTERN WALLFLOWER   MUSTARD FAMILY
Erysimum capitatum   *Cruciferae*
Habitat: dry gravelly or rocky places   June-August

This is a coarse plant 1'-2' tall with a dense raceme of strong yellow to deep orange flowers. This is a typical member of the mustard family as its flowers have the usual 4 petals that are positioned like a cross, 6 stamens, and alternate leaves. The petals of this species are about ½"-¾" long and its leaves, which are narrow and pointed, are 2"-3" long. There are usually small indentations along the margins of the leaves.
Type locality: Weaver Bally

121. STONECROP   STONECROP FAMILY
Sedum obtusatum ssp. *boreale*   *Crassulaceae*
Habitat: crevices of rocky cliffs or dry rocky slopes July

This stonecrop has a thick mat of succulent basal leaves up to 1" long that have rounded, slightly indented, blunt tips. There are much smaller leaves scattered along the stem. Numerous yellow flowers grow in a compact, somewhat flat-topped cluster at the end of a succulent stem 6" high. The leaves and stem, as well as the flower, sometimes take on a reddish tinge, especially with age. The petals are pointed, joined at the base, and about ⅓" long.
Type locality: Alpine Lake, Luella Lake

122. PURDY'S SEDUM   STONECROP FAMILY
Sedum purdyi   *Crassulareaceae*
Habitat: cliffs and rocky places   June

This succulent sedum has rosettes of flat yellow-green leaves less than 1" long. These differ greatly from the small oblong leaves that are scattered along the stem. The flowers are usually yellow and grow in compact clusters at the ends of erect stems about 6" tall. Each flower has 5 distinct petals about ¼" long.
Type locality: Canyon Creek, Hobo Gulch

123. KLAMATH WEED — ST. JOHNSWORT FAMILY

Hypericum perforatum — *Hypericaceae*
Habitat: dry fields and waste places, low elevations — July-August

This weed-like plant spreads easily and has become a pest in some areas. Its stems are tough, branched, and usually 2'-3' tall. It has opposite leaves that are narrowly oval and about 1" long. The flowers are in clusters at the ends of the several branchlets. There are 5 yellow petals ½" long and numerous erect stamens.
Type locality: Boulder Creek, Big Flat

124. GOLDEN-EYED GRASS — IRIS FAMILY

Sisyrinchium californicum — *Iridaceae*
Habitat: moist meadows — June

Although grass-like in appearance this is not a grass but a member of the Iris family and similar to the blue-eyed grass (see #254). The flowers are bright yellow and look like a 6-pointed star. The petals are about ½" long and have 5-7 parallel nerves or veins. The leaves and stems are thin and grass-like, about 1/8" wide.
Type locality: Lake Eleanor, Norwegian Meadow

125. MEADOW LOTUS — PEA FAMILY

Lotus oblongifolius — *Leguminoseae*
Habitat: moist places — June-July

This lotus is about 8"-16" tall and has pinnately compound leaves with elliptical leaflets 1" long. Most often there are 5 small pea-like yellow and white flowers growing together in a loose cluster in which all of the individual flower stems originate at one point forming an umbel. Immediately beneath this flower cluster is a green bract which looks very much like one of the leaflets.
Type locality: Norwegian Meadows, Boulder Creek

126. HILL LOTUS — PEA FAMILY

Lotus humistratus — *Leguminoseae*
Habitat: dry grassy slopes, lower elevations — April

This small, somewhat prostrate herb has stems which tend to turn upwards at the ends. The leaves are alternate and consist of usually 3 leaflets ¼"-½" long that are thickly covered with dense soft hairs. The small yellow pea-like flowers are about ¼" long and are borne singly in the axils of the leaves.
Type locality: Indian Creek

127. FALSE LUPINE — PEA FAMILY
Thermopsis gracilis — *Leguminoseae*
Habitat: open woods — June

This is called false lupine because of its similarity, at first glance, to the yellow lupine (see #130) but it is an entirely different genus. The most noticeable difference is the leaf which has only 3 leaflets. The individual flowers are larger and in a more lax cluster. Other botanical differences also exist.
Type locality: Boulder Creek, Granite Creek

128. YELLOW FAWN.LILY — LILY FAMILY
Erythronium grandiflorum var. *pallidum* — *Liliaceae*
Habitat: open woods or slopes — June

This member of the lily family has a single naked stem 8"-12" tall which rises directly from the ground between 2 clear green leaves 4"-8" long. The leaves are not mottled as in the white fawn lily (see #37). There are 2 to 5 nodding, golden yellow flowers. The petal-like flower segments are usually strongly recurved, 1"-1½" long. Emerging from the center are 6 conspicuous white stamens.
Type locality: Long Canyon

129. BOG-ASPHODEL — LILY FAMILY
Narthecium californicum — *Liliaceae*
Habitat: wet or boggy meadows — July

The slender erect stems of this plant are 1'-1½' tall and bear at their tip an elongated tight cluster of golden yellow flowers. The 6 petal-like parts of the flower are narrow and spreading, ¼"-⅓" long. An interesting characteristic of this plant are the filaments of the stamens which are wooly or hairy. The leaves are mostly basal and grass-like.
Type locality: Lake Eleanor, Mumford Meadows, Landers Meadows

130. YELLOW LUPINE — PEA FAMILY
Lupinus croceus — *Leguminoseae*
Habitat: dry woods and slopes — June

The erect stems of this lupine grow 1½'-2' tall and bear elongated clusters of bright yellow pea-like flowers. The leaves are palmately divided into 5-8 silky leaflets on a petiole 1"-3" long. The leaflets themselves are from 1½"-2½" long. These flowers make a bright splash of color among the dark greens of coniferous forests.
Type locality: Swift Creek, Long Canyon, Granite Creek

131. CHECKER-LILY
LILY FAMILY
Fritillaria lanceolata — *Liliaccae*
Habitat: open woods at lower elevations — May

This graceful plant has a slender stem up to 3' tall and has one to several nodding bell-shaped flowers. They vary in color from a pale greenish-yellow faintly mottled with purple to a brown-purple. The flower segments are from ¾"-1½" long and deeply bowl-shaped. Narrow leaves, 2"-5" long, grow in whorls on the upper stem.
Type locality: East Weaver Creek

132. BLAZING STAR
BLAZING STAR FAMILY
Mentzelia laevicaulis — *Loasaceae*
Habitat: dry places, disturbed soils — July

This is a stout plant 2'-3' high that has smooth, pale and shiny stems. Growing at the ends of the stems are 2 or 3 light yellow flowers that have 5 slender pointed petals, 2"-3" long, and numerous stamens almost as long as the petals.
Type locality: Helena

133. BROOM-RAPE
BROOM-RAPE FAMILY
Orobanche fasciculata — *Orobanchaceae*
Habitat: open forest, middle elevations — May

This is a parasite with no green leaves that lives on the roots of other plants. Several flower pedicels about 6" high grow, as in a bundle, from a succulent scaly stem. At the tip of each of these pedicels is a solitary, more or less 2-lipped, yellow flower tinged with purple that is about 1" long.
Type locality: Musser Hill, Weaver Bally

134. BUSH POPPY
POPPY FAMILY
Dendromecon rigida — *Papaveraceae*
Habitat: dry slopes, lower elevations — April

This is a rather stiff shrub about 3' tall with slender, pale green leaves that tend to orient themselves in a vertical position. Golden yellow flowers having 4 rounded petals about 1" long bloom singly at the ends of short branchlets.
Type locality: Lewiston Turnpike

135. CALIFORNIA POPPY — POPPY FAMILY
Eschscholzia californica — *Papaveraceae*
Habitat: grassy and open places, lower elevations — April-May

The conspicuous golden-yellow to orange flowers of this plant are recognized by their 4 petals, numerous stamens, and finely dissected leaves. Before the petals are open they are enclosed in a conical cap which splits and falls away as the petals unfold. Beneath the flower the flower-stalk is enlarged into a flat rim which is especially conspicuous after the petals have fallen.
Type locality: Weaverville

136. SULPHUR FLOWER — BUCKWHEAT FAMILY
Eriogonum umbellatum — *Polygonaceae*
Habitat: rocky soils, higher elevations — July-August

This is a very hardy, somewhat woody and branched plant from 5"-8" tall with conspicuous dense umbels of small sulphur yellow flowers that often take on a reddish tinge as they age. The small leaves, ½"-1" long, are green above and white-wooly beneath. This is an extremely variable species with many varieties having been identified.
Type locality: Horse Haven Meadows, Luella Lake, East Weaver Lake

137. SHRUBBY CINQUEFOIL — ROSE FAMILY
Potentilla fruticosa — *Rosaceae*
Habitat: open slopes — July

This is a low bushy shrub, usually about 2' high, with small leaves that are divided into 3-7 crowded narrow silky leaflets. Yellow flowers grow in small clusters at the tips of the branches or in the axils of the leaves. The petals are round, ¼"-½" long. As with other potentillas, there is a row of bracts immediately below and alternating with the sepals.
Type locality: Kidd Creek, Deadfall Lakes

138. WATER PLANTIAN BUTTERCUP — BUTTERCUP FAMILY
Ranunculus alismaefolius var. *hartwegii* — *Ranunculaceae*
Habitat: open damp rocky meadows — July

This small plant usually has several stems 3"-12" long with simple narrow leaves 1"-4" long, somewhat like those of the common plantian. The flowers usually occur in groups of three at the ends of each stem. There are 5 bright yellow petals about ⅓" long, greenish sepals, and numerous stamens.
Type locality: Landers Lake

139. STICKY CINQUEFOIL · ROSE FAMILY

Potentilla glandulosa ssp. *nevadensis* · *Rosaceae*
Habitat: open meadows and slopes · July

The slender stems of this plant are 8"-12" tall, somewhat reddish in color, and have mostly basal leaves that are pinnately divided into 5-9 sharply toothed leaflets. The potentillas have a row of bracts beneath the flower alternating with 5 pointed sepals. These sepals are usually visible between the petals when viewed from above. This helps distinguish it readily from the buttercups with which it might easily be confused by the casual observer. This is an extremely variable species.
Type locality: Sapphire Lake, Horse Haven Meadows

140. IVESIA · ROSE FAMILY

Ivesia gordonii · *Rosaceae*
Habitat: dry rocky places, higher elevations · July

Nearly leafless stems 2"-8" long bear crowded dense clusters of tiny yellow flowers. Triangular-shaped yellow sepals, 1/8" long, stand erect between yellow petals that are only half as long. The mostly basal leaves, 5"-7" long, are divided into numerous crowded pairs of cleft segments ¼" long.
Type locality: Diamond Lake-Summit Lake Divide

141. BIRD'S FOOT BUTTERCUP · BUTTERCUP FAMILY

Ranunculus orthorhynchus · *Ranunculaceae*
Habitat: meadows · June

The buttercups are easily identified by their shiny and waxy petals. Differences in the leaves and the type of seed largely differentiate the various species. The manner in which the leaflets are incised into sharply toothed segments gives this species its common name. The hollow, somewhat fleshy and hairy stems are 10"-20" long. The flowers have 5 golden yellow petals, 5 greenish-yellow sepals that are usually reflexed, and numerous stamens and pistils.
Type locality: Packer Meadow

142. SAXIFRAGE · SAXIFRAGE FAMILY

Saxifraga fragarioides · *Saxifragaceae*
Habitat: rock ledges and crevices · July

This is a stout plant with stems 4"-8" high having mostly basal leaves ½"-1½" long. The leaves are somewhat wedge-shaped, narrow at the

bottom, and wider and toothed at the tip. The flower stem is narrowly branched and bears compact clusters of tiny flowers on each branchlet. There is a yellow appearance to the flowers because of the many yellow stamens that are more conspicuous than its tiny white petals that are only 1/16" long.
Type locality: Caribou Lake

143. COMMON MONKEY-FLOWER — FIGWORT FAMILY
Mimulus guttatus — *Scrophulareaceae*
Habitat: wet places — July

This extremely variable species is from 1'-3' tall. It has opposite oval leaves 1" long that are slightly toothed. The flowers are tubular, 2-lipped, and with a constricted throat that is nearly closed by 2 heavy ridges on the lower lip. They are bright yellow in color with red spots in the throat and are about 1" long. A small and delicate variety of this species (*Mimulus guttatus* var. *micranthus*) has stems 2"-4" tall and flowers about ½" long. This has been observed in the Kidd Creek Basin.
Type locality: Lake Eleanor, Big Flat, Deer Creek, Swift Creek

144. PRIMROSE MIMULUS — FIGWORT FAMILY
Mimulus primuloides var. *linearifolius* — *Scrophulareaceae*
Habitat: meadows — June-August

The slender stem of this plant usually bears one, more or less erect flower. The flowers are yellow with an open throat, ¾"-1" long, and are borne on slender stems nearly 3" long. This is a variable species. In this variety the leaves are narrow, ¾"-2" long, and usually crowded at the base.
Type locality: Preacher Meadow, Deer Creek Meadow, Gulick Creek Basin

145. COBWEBBY INDIAN PAINT-BRUSH — FIGWORT FAMILY
Castilleja arachnoidea — *Scrophulareaceae*
Habitat: open dry slopes — August

This plant usually has several leafy stems 4"-10" tall. The leaves are somewhat wooly, very slender, up to 1½" long and may have 1 or 2 spreading lobes. Like other paint-brushes, the flowers are in compact spikes at the ends of the stems. Greenish or yellowish bracts hide the whitish or pale yellow flowers which are about ½" long.
Type locality: Luella Lake, Kidd Creek

146. HAIRY PRIMROSE MIMULUS or CANDELABRUM MIMULUS

FIGWORT FAMILY
Schrophulareaceae

Mimulus primuloides var. *pilosellus*
June
Habitat: wet meadows

The leaves distinguish this variety of the primrose mimulus. They are oval, 1" long, crowded, and are covered with long, soft white hairs which catch the dew and glisten in the sun. The flowers, borne on slender stems, are yellow with red spots, funnelform in shape, and about ⅓" long.
Type locality: Packer Meadow

147. CANDELABRUM MONKEY-FLOWER

FIGWORT FAMILY
Scrophulareaceae

Mimulus pulsiferae
Habitat: moist gravelly places
May

This is a small delicate mimulus 2"-6" high with slightly sticky herbage. The leaves, which have a tendency to be somewhat purplish, are about ½" long and are in pairs widely spaced on the stem. The flowers are funnel-like, about ⅓" long, with 5 unequal spreading lobes that are yellow and have red markings or spots on the lower throat.
Type locality: Weaver Bally

148. MUSK FLOWER

FIGWORT FAMILY
Scrophulareaceae

Mimulus moschatus
Habitat: moist soil or along stream banks
July-August

This is a hairy and somewhat slimy plant 2"-12" tall. Its opposite leaves are finely toothed and ½"-1½" long. The yellow flowers are funnel-shaped with an open throat and spreading rounded lobes. They are ¾"-1" long and are borne in the axils of the leaves on a slender flower-stalk 1"-2" long.
Type locality: Horse Haven Meadows, Lake Anna

149. HOT-ROCK PENSTEMON

FIGWORT FAMILY
Scrophulareaceae

Penstemon deustus
Habitat: dry rocky slopes
July

The erect woody stems of this plant are from 8"-24" tall and terminate in an elongated spike-like cluster of buff-colored flowers marked with purple lines. The flowers are 2-lipped, less than 1" long, with the upper lip being shorter than the lower. The middle lobe of the 3-lobed lower lip is the broadest. The stems are leafy with many pairs of opposite leaves up to 1½" long that are oval in outline, pointed at the tip, and with coarsely toothed margins.
Type locality: Alpine Lake Trail

150. COMMON MULLEIN   FIGWORT FAMILY
Verbascum thapsus   *Scrophulareaceae*
Habitat: dry sandy places, disturbed soils   July-August

There is a weed-like aspect to this plant for it frequently occupies waste places. Its 6' tall stem rises from a basal rosette of wooly leaves. This rosette elongates as the stem grows. At the tip of the stem is a long, thick floral spike of yellow flowers that open in an irregular order as the stem grows. Each flower is about 1" across and has 5 nearly equal petals.
Type locality: Big Flat, Adams Lake Trail, Boulder Creek

151. SIERRA SANICLE   PARSLEY FAMILY
Sanicula graveolens   *Umbelliferae*
Habitat: dry open flats   June

Members of the parsley family are characterized by the manner in which the flowers grow in their cluster. In this case the stems (rays) of the flowers all radiate out from a common spot very much as do the ribs of an umbrella (an umbel). In this species there are 3-5 rays, each with 10-15 tiny yellow flowers. The plant is low and spreading. It has somewhat purplish stems 2"-10" long with leaves 1½" long, that are lobed and incised into several segments. The turkey-pea, *Sanicula tuberosa*, is a similar species growing in the same area. Its leaves are much more finely divided into many narrow feathery segments.
Type locality: Big Flat

152. YELLOW OWL'S CLOVER   FIGWORT FAMILY
or CUTLEAF ORTHOCARPUS
Orthocarpus lacerus   *Scrophulareaceae*
Habitat: grassy slopes and swales   June

The slender stems of this plant are 3"-8" long and end in a loose cluster of lemon yellow flowers. The flowers are about ½" long and are 2-lipped, the upper lip being straight and the lower lip inflated into what appears to be 3 sac-like lobes. The leaves are very narrow with the upper ones being divided into 3-7 extremely narrow segments.
Type locality: Trinity Center

153. STREAM VIOLET

Viola glabella
Habitat: wet woods and stream banks

VIOLET FAMILY
Violaceae
May

The thin heart-shaped leaves of this violet are bright green in color and have long petioles. Most of the leaves are near the upper end of the stem. The flowers are a clear yellow with some purple veining on the front of the lower petals. The upper petals are yellow on the back side in contrast to the other species illustrated here which have a brownish or purplish color on the backs of the upper petals.
Type locality: French Creek

154. MOUNTAIN VIOLET

Viola purpurea
Habitat: dry rocky slopes

VIOLET FAMILY
Violaceae
May

The leaves of this violet are often somewhat purplish in color. They are oval or egg-shaped, tapering to a petiole at the base and narrowing towards the tip. The margins have irregular and shallowly rounded teeth. The flowers are a deep yellow with brownish veins on the lower petals and purplish coloring on the backs of the upper petals.
Type locality: Weaver Bally, Boulder Creek, Hobo Gulch

155. SHELTON'S VIOLET

Viola sheltonii
Habitat: open woods

VIOLET FAMILY
Violaceae
June

Leaves that are twice dissected palmately into narrow segments distinguishes this violet from the others. The leaves are broader than they are long and have a whitish cast to their dark green color. The flowers are lemon-yellow with brownish lines on the 3 lower petals. There is a brownish-purple color to the backs of the 2 upper petals.
Type locality: Packer Meadow, Upper Clear Creek

156. PINE VIOLET

Viola lobata
Habitat: open woods

VIOLET FAMILY
Violaceae
June

This violet stands erect on stems 4"-12" long. The leaves are mostly on the upper part of the stem and are irregularly lobed into several finger-like segments. The flowers are a deep lemon-yellow with a few brown veins near the base of the petals and a brownish tinge on the backs of the upper petals.
Type locality: Boulder Creek

157. MOUNTAIN DOGBANE   **DOGBANE FAMILY**
Apocynum pumilum   *Apocynaceae*
Habitat: dry rocky slopes   July-August

This is a low, branching and spreading plant with drooping, opposite, oblong-oval leaves that are green above and pale beneath. Abundant pink flowers nearly cover the plant. They are cylindrical in shape with 5 reflexed lobes, pale in color. The plant freely secretes an abundant milky juice if broken.
Type locality: Boulder Creek, Horse Haven Meadow

158. PURPLE MILKWEED   **MILKWEED FAMILY**
Asclepias cordifolia   *Asclepiadaceae*
Habitat: dry rocky or open wooded slopes   June

This milkweed has broad heart-shaped leaves about 6" long that clasp the stem. Numerous flowers are clustered together in loose umbels. They have 5 dark reddish-purple, strongly reflexed lobes and a central conical crown that is noticeably paler.
Type locality: Backbone Creek, Weaver Bally

159. COMMON MILKWEED   **MILKWEED FAMILY**
Asclepias speciosa   *Asclepiadaceae*
Habitat: gravelly or sandy places, lower elevations   June

This milkweed has erect stout stems 2'-4' tall with thick, wooly, oblong leaves 4"-6" long. The flowers grow in round compact clusters at the ends of the stems. The individual flower has 5 reflexed rose-purple concave lobes, ⅓" long, and a pinkish to yellowish "crown" in the center. The stems contain an abundance of milky juice.
Type locality: Weaverville, Norwegian Meadow

160. SWAMP ONION   **AMARYLLIS FAMILY**
Allium vallidum   *Amaryllidaceae*
Habitat: wet places   July-August

Usually growing in large clumps or colonies, this sturdy onion is 1½'-3' tall. It has 3-5 broad green leaves 1'-2' long. The compact flower heads have rose colored flowers about ½" long. Its 6 stamens and slender style are often conspicuously exserted beyond the segments giving it a fluffy appearance.
Type locality: Echo Lake, Seven-up Lake, Horse Haven Meadows

161. SCYTHE-LEAVED ONION — AMARYLLIS FAMILY
Allium falcifolium — *Amaryllidaceae*
Habitat: dry sandy flats, rocky soil — July

This low onion seems to hug the ground for its short flattened flowering stem is only 2"-4" long, shorter than its 2 sickle-shaped leaves. The compact flower head has rose to purple flowers. The individual flowers have short stems ¼"-½" long and narrow, pointed flower segments that are erect and about ½" long.
Type locality: Caribou Trail

162. FIRE-CRACKER FLOWER — AMARYLLIS FAMILY
Brodiaea ida-maia — *Amaryllidaceae*
Habitat: open woods, lower elevations — May

The stiff erect leafless stem of this unusual flower is 1'-3' tall and bears a tight cluster of 6-12 pendulous flowers. The flower consists of a broad scarlet tube about 1" long with very short greenish lobes at the tip. These recurve backwards at maturity exposing white sterile stamens. There are 3 grass-like leaves 1'-1½' long.
Type locality: French Creek, Oregon Mountain

163. WESTERN HOUND'S TONGUE — BORAGE FAMILY
Cynoglossum occidentale — *Boraginaceae*
Habitat: dry open slopes — May-June

This is a hairy plant with an erect stem 1'-1½' tall bearing long slender leaves and a terminal cluster of small bluish-brownish-reddish flowers ¼" long. The fruit, which is the plant's most distinctive feature, is a roundish nutlet, ⅓" in diameter, covered with bristly barbs.
Type locality: Yellow Rose Trail, Tannery Gulch

164. TWINFLOWER — HONEYSUCKLE FAMILY
Linnaea borealis ssp. *longiflora* — *Caprifoliaceae*
Habitat: dense woods — June

This is a weak trailing plant that often carpets the forest floor. Its leaves are opposite, shiny, and slightly toothed. Bell-like flowers grow in symmetrical pairs at the tip of an erect slender forked stem 2"-3" tall.
Type locality: Boulder Creek, Stuarts Fork

165. CREEPING SNOWBERRY
Symphoricarpus mollis
Habitat: shaded slopes

HONEYSUCKLE FAMILY
Caprifoliaceae
June

This species of snowberry is a spreading plant about 1' high with weak, vine-like trailing stems. The opposite leaves are thin, oval, and about ½"-¾" long. Small pink flowers usually appear in pairs but are inconspicuous. By August they have developed into globular fleshy white fruits about ¼" in diameter. (See also #166.)
Type locality: Boulder Creek

166. COMMON SNOWBERRY
Symphoricarpus rivularis
Habitat: canyon banks near streams, lower elevations

HONEYSUCKLE FAMILY
Caprifoliaceae
June

This species is an erect shrub 2'-5' tall with slender branches which have small, opposite, oval leaves 1"-1½" long. Several small pinkish, bell-shaped flowers, ¼" long, hang in a cluster at the ends of the small branches. More conspicuous than the flowers are the globose fleshy white fruits. These are ½" in diameter. (See also #165.)
Type locality: Norwegian Meadow

167. MOUNTAIN DAISY
or DAISY-FLEABANE
Erigeron peregrinus ssp. *callianthemus*
Habitat: small streamsides, moist meadows

SUNFLOWER FAMILY
Compositae
July-August

The simple stem of this daisy-like plant usually bears a single showy flower 1"-2" across that contains many rose-purple petal-like ray flowers and a center of yellow disc flowers. The narrow leaves are up to 4" long and ¾" wide and grow mostly on the lower half of the stem.
Type locality: Horse Haven Meadow, Kidd Creek

168. ROSY EVERLASTING
Antennaria rosea
Habitat: dry forest openings

SUNFLOWER FAMILY
Compositae
June

Rosy colored dry bracts surround each flower head making this small everlasting easy to identify. The plant is white-wooly and has several stems 2"-10" tall, forming a mat. There are many narrow basal leaves about 1" long as well as narrower leaves scattered along the stem. The flowers are grouped in one or more compact heads at the tips of the stems.
Type locality: Big Flat

169. INDIAN CARTWHEEL   PINK FAMILY
Silene hookeri   *Caryophyllaceae*
Habitat: dry rocky ground, open hillsides   May-June

The showy flowers of this plant are 1"-2" across and have 5 pink or white petals standing out at right angles. The petals are slashed into 4 narrow lobes, the middle two lobes being larger than the lateral ones. (See #6 for a subspecies in which the lobes are all equal and nearly twice the size.) The stems are 3"-5" high with leaves that are grayish-green, narrowly oval, 1"-2" long and ½" wide. The name "pink" given to this family refers to the slashed margins of the petals and also relates it to pinking shears used for making jagged cuts.
Type locality: Norwegian Meadow

170. WILD GINGER   BIRTHWORT FAMILY
Asarum caudatum   *Aristolochiaceae*
Habitat: deep shade   May

The trailing rootstalks of the wild ginger bear pairs of dark green heart-shaped leaves 2"-6" broad which make a lush ground cover in the shade of damp woods. The flowers are very inconspicuous as they are dark brown and hidden beneath the leaves close to the ground. There are no petals. Its 3 sepals form into long tapering lobes looking very much like a mouse's tail or a spider's leg.
Type locality: Boulder Creek, Stuarts Fork

171. BREWER'S THISTLE   SUNFLOWER FAMILY
Cirsium brewerii   *Compositae*
Habitat: wet places   July

This is a slender white-wooly thistle 3' tall with a simple stem which is branched above. The leaves are irregularly lobed and tipped with strong spines. The flower heads are about 1" high and have a cylindrical or globular whorl of bracts beneath that have weak spines and a dark spot at their tips. The flowers are a pink or pale purple and are usually crowded together in a compact group.
Type locality: Swift Creek

172. BULL THISTLE   SUNFLOWER FAMILY
Cirsium vulgare   *Compositae*
Habitat: waste places   August

This is a very coarse thistle 2'-4' tall usually growing in disturbed soils. The leaves are long, coarsely toothed and covered with long sharp prick-

les. The flower heads which are up to 1½" in diameter have a globular whorl of sharp needle-like bracts. The flowers are a clear, striking rose-purple color.
Type locality: Big Flat

173. ANDERSON'S THISTLE — SUNFLOWER FAMILY
Cirsium andersonii — *Compositae*
Habitat: dry slopes — August

This thistle has a slender, sparingly branched, reddish stem nearly 3' tall and usually bears one flower head of rose-purple flowers. The upper stem is nearly leafless with its long, narrow, pinnately lobed leaves restricted to the lower half of the stem.
Type locality: Scott Mountain

174. TOOTHWORT or MILK-MAIDS — MUSTARD FAMILY
Dentaria californica — *Cruciferae*
Habitat: shady banks, lower elevations — March

This is one of the earliest flowers to appear in the spring. The slender erect stems are from 4"-10" long with 1 or 2 basal leaves that have 3 oval to roundish leaflets. Upper leaves along the stem have 3-5 long, narrow leaflets or lobes. The flowers have 4 pale rose to lavender petals ⅓"-½" long. They quickly develop into fruiting pods 1"-2" long and 1/8" broad.
Type locality: Big Bar

175. PINK MOUNTAIN HEATHER — HEATHER FAMILY
Phyllodoce empetriformis — *Ericaceae*
Habitat: rocky slopes at higher elevations — July

This is a woody plant up to 1' tall. Its evergreen leaves are crowded and needle-like, ½" long. Rose-red flowers are bell-shaped, ¼" long, and grow in crowded clusters at the ends of the branches.
Type locality: Lake Anna, Grizzly Lake

176. GREENLEAF MANZANITA — HEATHER FAMILY
Arctostaphyllos patula — *Ericaceae*
Habitat: dry open slopes — June

This is a stout shrub 3'-6' tall with a coarsely branching structure. There are many rigid, smooth, reddish-brown branches with broadly oval evergreen leaves 1"-1½" long. Numerous deep pink, urn-shaped

flowers ¼" long hang in very dense clusters on many small branchlets. The fruits are very dark, blackish berries about ⅓" in diameter.
Type locality: Union Lake Trail, Rush Creek Trail

177. BLEEDING HEART
Dicentra formosa
Habitat: damp shaded places

BLEEDING HEART FAMILY
Fumariaceae
June

This plant has slender stems 1'-1½' tall and basal leaves that are 3 times finely dissected so as to appear somewhat fern-like. Nodding or pendant pink flowers about ¾" long resemble a flattened heart with a crack in it.
Type locality: Boulder Creek, Battle Creek, South Fork Mountain

178. REDBUD
Cercis occidentalis
Habitat: dry slopes and canyons, lower elevations

PEA FAMILY
Leguminoseae
April

This is a colorful deciduous shrub 6'-15' tall. The roundish leaves are heart-shaped, palmately veined, 1"-3" broad. Pinkish to magenta pea-like flowers appear before the leaves have fully developed. Conspicuous oblong, flat, bean-like seedpods are pendant and frequently persistent on the shrub. They are often reddish-purple in color and up to 3½" long.
Type locality: along the Trinity River

179. BROAD-LEAVED LOTUS
Lotus crassifolius
Habitat: dry slopes, middle elevations

PEA FAMILY
Leguminoseae
May

This lotus has hollow stems and its leaves have 7-15 leaflets up to 1" long. There are 8-15 slender yellowish flowers, marked with dark red, that are closely grouped in a one-sided cluster. These pea-like flowers are about ½" long and develop into brownish or reddish pods up to 2" long.
Type locality: Granite Lake Trail, Buckhorn Mountain

180. SHASTA CLOVER
Trifolium productum
Habitat: damp places, high elevations

PEA FAMILY
Leguminoseae
July

The 3 leaflets of this clover are long-oval and have toothed margins. They are ½"-1½" long and taper to a point at the apex. The individual rose to purple flowers in the compact flower head are about ½" long and reflex downward soon after developing.
Type locality: Sunrise Pass, Luella Lake

181. SCARLET FRITILLARY   LILY FAMILY
Fritillaria recurva   *Liliaceae*
Habitat: dry woods   May

This plant is easy to recognize by its nodding, bell-like scarlet flowers which tend to turn to one side of a stem 1'-3' tall. The tips of the flower segments are curled back; the interior of the flower is spotted with yellow; and long, narrow, pointed leaves up to 4" long usually grow in 2 or 3 whorls along the central portion of the stem.
Type locality: Backbone Creek, Coffee Creek, Weaver Bally

182. GIANT HYSSOP or HORSE MINT   MINT FAMILY
Agastache urticifolia   *Labiatae*
Habitat: damp places, middle elevations   July

This is a tall member of the mint family with square stems and opposite, coarsely toothed leaves 1¼"-3" long. The flowers are 2-lipped, pale rose to lavender, and crowded into a terminal spike 2"-6" long. As with all mints, there are 4 stamens but with this species the upper pair of stamens are longer than the lower pair.
Type locality: Horse Haven Meadows, Caribou Trail

183. LEOPARD LILY (TIGER LILY)   LILY FAMILY
Lilium pardalinum   *Liliaceae*
Habitat: stream banks, wet places   June-July

This lily grows to a height of 8'. The leaves are 3"-7" long and 1" wide with 9 or more leaves growing in whorls widely scattered along the stem. The flower segments are reddish—orange at the tip and yellow-orange with maroon dots near the base. The segments are 2" or more long and strongly recurved. The anthers are nearly ½" long and hang down conspicuously from the center of the nodding flowers. A similar species (*Lilium kelleyanum*) also occurs in the Trinity mountains. In general it is smaller in size with 8 or less leaflets in a whorl and flower segments that are 2" or less in length.
Type locality: Stuarts Fork, Norwegian Meadow, Canyon Creek

184. ROSE EPILOBIUM   EVENING PRIMROSE FAMILY
or ROCK FRINGE   *Onagraceae*
Epilobium obcordatum   July
Habitat: rocky slopes, high elevations

This is a low plant with spreading leafy stems about 6" long. The broad leaves are opposite, crowded, 1"-2" long. Showy rose-purple flowers

borne singly in the axils of the upper leaves have 4 petals that are heart-shaped and about ½" long.
Type locality: Lake Anna, Black Basin

185. MOUNTAIN RED ELDER-BERRY (fruit)

HONEYSUCKLE FAMILY
Caprifoliaceae

Sambucus microbotrys August
Habitat: moist places and stream banks, higher elevations

This is a rounded shrub 2'-6' tall with dome shaped clusters of tiny creamy white flowers. These develop into showy clusters of red berries 1/16" in diameter. The leaves are pinnately divided into 5-7 leaflets 1¼"-3" long with coarsely toothed margins.
Type locality: Kidd Creek, Alpine Lake

186. OREGON SIDALCEA

MALLOW FAMILY
Malvaceae

Sidalcea oregana
Habitat: dry rocky meadows June-July

This is a very diverse species with several varieties named, based on minute botanical differences. The leaves are round in outline, shallowly lobed when at the base of the stem and more deeply lobed or incised if along the upper stem. The flowers occur in elongated clusters that sometimes are very dense and at other times are open and loose. They have 5 light to deep-pink petals ½"-¾" long and stamens that are compressed together into a tube around the pistil.
Type locality: Deer Creek, Big Flat, Norwegian Meadow

187. STRIPED CORAL-ROOT

ORCHID FAMILY
Orchidaceae

Corallorhiza striata
Habitat: shaded woods June

This is a parasite with no green leaves. It draws its nourishment from roots of other plants or from decaying organic matter. Its red stem is 1'-1½' tall with the leaves reduced to sheathing scales along the stem. Pinkish-yellow or whitish flowers, striped with red, grow in an elongated spike-like cluster. The petal-like flower segments are about ⅓" long.
Type locality: South Fork of the Salmon

188. CALYPSO ORCHID — ORCHID FAMILY
Calypso bulbosa — *Orchidaceae*
Habitat: forest leaf mold — May

This pretty orchid grows singly at the tip of a naked reddish stem about 6" long. There is but one basal egg-shaped leaf, 1¼"-2½" long. The flowers, which bear a similarity to the lady-slipper, have rose colored petals and sepals ½"-¾" long. The lower lip is sac-like and about ¾" long. It is white and streaked or spotted with a brownish or red-purple color.
Type locality: Boulder Creek

189. SPOTTED CORAL-ROOT — ORCHID FAMILY
Corallorhiza maculata — *Orchidaceae*
Habitat: dry shaded woods — June-July

This parasitic plant has a brownish-purple or yellowish stem up to 2' tall. Orchid-like flowers having a distinctive pointed spur are scattered along the upper end of the stem. The flowers are reddish-purple to greenish in color. The lower lip is white and spotted or veined with red and has 2 small lateral lobes.
Type locality: Boulder Creek, Long Canyon, Section-line Lake

190. CLARKIA or RED RIBBONS EVENING PRIMROSE FAMILY
Clarkia concinna — *Onagraceae*
Habitat: dry loose soil, lower elevations — June

This herb may have a single stem or be freely branching, ½'-2' high. Its leaves are narrowly oval, 1"-2" long. The flowers are a blending of rose-pink, red-pink, and white. Its 4 petals are cleft into 3 nearly equal narrow lobes with the middle one slightly longer than the lateral ones.
Type locality: Weaver Bally, Big Bar

191. CALIFORNIA GROUND CONE — BROOM-RAPE FAMILY
Boschniakia strobilacea — *Orobanchaceae*
Habitat: dry areas in company with manzanita or madrone — June

This is a parasitic herb growing primarily on the roots of manzanita or madrone. The stem is 1½"-2½" thick and covered with dark brown bracts which gives it the appearance of a pine cone. Almost hidden by the bracts are small tubular 2-lipped flowers, the lower lip having 3 lobes. Its 4 cream colored stamens are conspicuous against the dark coloring of the rest of the plant.
Type locality: Pony Mountain

192. STREAM ORCHID

Epipactis gigantea

Habitat: streambanks and areas around springs

ORCHID FAMILY

Orchidaceae

June

The leafy stems of this orchid reach 3' in height and bear in the axils of the leaves orchid-like flowers that have 3 spreading coppery-green sepals about 1" long. The petals are reddish, veined with purple, the lower one having a hinged portion that is yellowish and looks like a tongue. The leaves, 3"-8" long, are alternate and oval and clasp the stem.

Type locality: Norwegian Meadows

193. FIREWEED

Epilobium angustifolium

Habitat: burned over or logged areas, damp forest openings

EVENING PRIMROSE FAMILY

Onagraceae

August

The rose-pink flowers of this showy plant are borne on an elongated flower-stalk. Because the lower flowers bloom first the flower cluster often takes on the appearance of a tapering spire. The stems are 3' or more tall and bear opposite, slender leaves about 5" long which resemble the leaves of the willow. There are 4 petals, 4 sepals and 8 stamens.

Type locality: Alpine Lake, Granite Lake Trail

194. NARROW-LEAVED COLLOMIA

Collomia linearis

Habitat: dry open slopes

PHLOX FAMILY

Polemoniaceae

June

The simple erect, sometimes branched, stem of this annual is from 4"-16" tall and bears at its tip a head-like cluster of small pinkish, funnel-shaped flowers about ½" long. Its alternate leaves, which are up to 2" long, are narrow and usually pointed. Leaf-like bracts are beneath the flower clusters.

Type locality: Upper South Fork of the Salmon

195. BRIGHT COLLOMIA

Collomia tinctoria

Habitat: dry rocky slopes

PHLOX FAMILY

Polemoniaceae

May-June

This is a low sticky plant 3"-6" high with narrow leaves that taper at each end. The flowers are in small clusters at the ends of the stems. One or two blossoms may grow in the axils of the small branches. Each blossom is like a slender funnel ½" long, the tube being red-violet and the lobes pale pink.

Type locality: Weaver Bally

196. VARIABLE-LEAVED COLLOMIA   PHLOX FAMILY
Collomia heterophylla   *Polemoniaceae*
Habitat: disturbed soils, low elevations   May

This is a low, branched, sticky annual 2"-8" tall. Its leaves are variable in shape and usually toothed or cleft. They are broader in outline than those of our other collomias. The flowers are tubular, about ½" long, with 5 short pale pink lobes.
Type locality: Weaver Bally, Boulder Creek

197. LARGE-FLOWERED COLLOMIA   PHLOX FAMILY
Collomia grandiflora   *Polemoniaceae*
Habitat: dry open slopes and meadows   July

The stems of this plant are simple and erect, ½'-3' tall, and bear slender leaves 1"-2" long. The flowers are pale salmon, about 1" long, and grow in compact head-like clusters at the ends of the stems. The narrow funnel-form of the flower tube and its 5 spreading lobes give the appearance of a bursting rocket.
Type locality: Caribou Trail

198. WILLOW-HERB   EVENING PRIMROSE FAMILY
Epilobium sp.   *Onagraceae*
Habitat: wet or damp ground   July-August

Several species of willow-herb with but small botanical differences grow in this area. The small flowers all have 4 petals with each petal notched so as to appear to be 4 pairs of petals. They are often pink to purplish (or whitish) in color. There are 4 sepals and 8 stamens. The ovary is below the flower and is greatly elongated.
Type locality: Long Canyon

199. SPREADING PHLOX   PHLOX FAMILY
Phlox diffusa   *Polemoniaceae*
Habitat: open rocky places, higher elevations   July

The stems of this plant are densely tufted, covered with short pointed leaves, and form thick moss-like mats 4"-6" high. The flowers bloom so thickly that they almost hide the leaves. The petals vary from white to pink to lavender and have rounded lobes ¼" long that spread abruptly at right angles to the tube of the flower.
Type locality: Caribou Lakes, Yellow Rose Mine

200. SHOWY PHLOX — PHLOX FAMILY

Phlox speciosa var. *occidentalis* — *Polemoniaceae*

Habitat: rocky hillsides and wooded slopes — May

The flowers of this species are twice the size of those of the spreading phlox (see #199). The petals are a bright pink and usually have a notch in the center of each lobe. Several woody stems branch from near the base. Its narrow leaves are opposite, ½"-2" long and ¼"-⅓" wide.
Type locality: Musser Hill, Billy's Peak

201. HENDERSON'S SHOOTING STAR — PRIMROSE FAMILY

Dodecatheon hendersonii — *Primulaceae*

Habitat: open woods — May-June

This species is found at lower elevations than the Jeffrey's shooting star (see #202). It has a rosette of basal leaves that are roundish to oval and 1"-2" long. The flowering stem is 6"-14" high and bears a small cluster of flowers having magenta or deep lavender reflexed petals and a central column of very dark stamens.
Type locality: Big Flat, Musser Hill

202. JEFFREY'S SHOOTING STAR — PRIMROSE FAMILY

Dodecatheon jeffreyi — *Primulaceae*

Habitat: wet places — July-August

The petals of the shooting star bend back sharply exposing dark stamens that are so close together that they look like a cone with the style projecting out from its center. With this species the leaves are 2"-15" long, about 1" wide, and stand erect. The leafless flower stalk is from 9"-24" long and bears 3-18 purplish-lavender flowers. There is a maroon and yellow ring at the base of the petals.
Type locality: Kidd Creek, Section-line Lake

203. DWARF MINER'S LETTUCE — PURSLANE FAMILY

Montia perfoliata var. *depressa* — *Portulacaceae*

Habitat: dry shaded slopes, middle elevations — May

This is another of the many varieties of miner's lettuce (see #61 and #62). This is a very small, depressed form that is 1"-5" high and often a very definite orange-red color. The 2 upper leaves are sometimes joined into only a partial disc. The basal leaves are broader than long.
Type locality: Hayfork

204. PUSSY PAWS
Calyptridium umbellatum
Habitat: dry sandy or gravelly places

PURSLANE FAMILY
Portulacaceae
June-July

The name given this plant describes this flower well for the densely crowded flowers do look and feel like a cat's paw. The leafless stems, 2"-6" long, bear dull white to pink flowers 1/8"-1/4" long. The leaves, which have a leathery texture, are mostly basal, 1"-2" long, and widest at the tip. Both the leaves and the reddish stems tend to hug the ground during the cool parts of the day, but during the heat of midday they stand more or less upright.
Type locality: Alpine Lake, Long Canyon, Big Flat

205. SISKIYOU LEWISIA
Lewisia cotyledon
Habitat: rocky places and cliffs

PURSLANE FAMILY
Portulacaceae
July

The flowering stem of this lewisia is about 12" long and bears large clusters of showy flowers. Each flower has 5-10 white petals that are striped with red and about ½" long. The numerous leaves are fleshy and broad, up to 4" long, and primarily occur as a basal rosette. A variety of this species, Heckner's lewisia (*Lewisia cotyledon* var. *heckneri*) found on Weaver Bally Mountain has leaves with margins that are indented or toothed instead of plain and petals that are about ¼" longer.
Type locality: Alpine Lake, Caribou Trail

206. COLUMBIA LEWISIA
Lewisia columbiana
Habitat: rocky slopes

PURSLANE FAMILY
Portulacaceae
July

The several flowering stems of this succulent plant are about 8" tall and bear loose clusters of rose colored flowers ⅓" long. There is sometimes a darker line down the mid-rib of the petals. Numerous narrow, fleshy, somewhat flattened leaves 2"-4" long form a basal tuft.
Type locality: Long Canyon, Alpine Lake

207. LEE'S LEWISIA
Lewisia leana
Habitat: rocky places

PURSLANE FAMILY
Portulacaceae
July

The fleshy leaves of this lewisia are 1"-2½" long. They are very narrow, roundish in cross section, and grow in dense tufts at the base of the flowering stem. The flowers grow in a loosely branched cluster. There are 6-8, mostly pink, petals about ¼" long.
Type locality: Alpine Lake

208. SCARLET GILIA   PHLOX FAMILY
Gilia aggregata   *Polemoniaceae*
Habitat: dry open slopes   July

The simple sticky stem of this plant is about 2' tall and bears scarlet-red flowers that usually stand at right angles along one side of the upper portion of the stem. The flowers resemble a narrow trumpet 1" long which bursts into a 5-pointed star. It has glossy flat green leaves 1"-2" long that are pinnately dissected into narrow segments.
Type locality: Long Canyon, Big Flat

209. STAR-FLOWER   PRIMROSE FAMILY
Trientalis latifolia   *Primulaceae*
Habitat: forest shade   June

A single erect stem 4"-8" long bears a whorl of broad oval leaves from the center of which rises 1-4 delicate flower stems, each bearing a single star-shaped flower. The flower is about ½" across and is deeply parted into 5-7 delicate pink, sharply pointed, segments.
Type locality: Coffee Creek

210. SIERRA PRIMROSE   PRIMROSE FAMILY
Primula suffrutescens   *Primulaceae*
Habitat: near receding snowbanks at higher elevations   August

The striking rose colored flowers of this small plant have a yellow throat at the base of 5 spreading, notched petals. The flowers grow in small clusters on leafless stems 3"-4" high. Leaves are evergreen, wedge-shaped, toothed at the tip, 1" long, and crowded on short stems.
Type locality: Thompson Peak

211. PINE-DROPS   WINTERGREEN FAMILY
Pterospora andromedea   *Pyrolaceae*
Habitat: shaded woods   July

This is a saprophyte which gets its nourishment from decaying organic matter in the soil. It has erect simple reddish stems 1'-3' tall with small brown scales instead of green leaves. Numerous urn-shaped flowers hang pendulous along the upper half of the stem. They are white to reddish when young and dry brown with age.
Type locality: Swift Creek, Boulder Creek, Deadfall Lakes

212. LITTLE PRINCE'S PINE
Chimaphila menziesii
Habitat: shaded woods

WINTERGREEN FAMILY
Pyrolaceae
July

The stout erect stems of this species are about 6" high with a few simple leathery leaves ½"-2" long. The leaves are somewhat oval in shape and wider than those of the regular prince's pine (see #215). There are from 1-3 flowers whose petals spread widely exposing a large blunt stigma in the center.
Type locality: Kidd Creek Trail

213. LEAFLESS PYROLA
Pyrola picta forma *aphylla*
Habitat: rich forest humus

WINTERGREEN FAMILY
Pyrolaceae
July

This is a parasitic plant that usually has no green leaves but lives on the roots of other plants. The leaves are reduced to scale-like reddish bracts on reddish stems 7"-14" tall. The flowers are nodding and have 5 cup-shaped concave thick pinkish petals.
Type locality: Boulder Creek

214. MILKWORT
Polygala cornuta
Habitat: rocky or gravelly slopes

MILKWORT FAMILY
Polygalaceae
August

Although the casual observer might at first think this to be a member of the pea family its structure differs greatly from it. This plant has 5 sepals, 2 of which look like plum colored wings. There are but 3 petals. They are yellowish or greenish-white in color and are partially united to enclose the stamens and pistil. The stems are up to 12" long with leaves that are long-oval and up to 1¼" long.
Type locality: Kidd Creek, Minersville

215. PIPSISSEWA
or PRINCE'S PINE
Chimaphila umbellata var. *occidentalis*
Habitat: dry wooded slopes

WINTERGREEN FAMILY
Pyrolaceae
June-July

This low growing plant is about 12" tall and spreads by a creeping underground rootstalk. Its evergreen leathery leaves are narrow with finely toothed margins and about 3" long. The leaves appear to grow in whorls. The 3-7 nodding flowers have 5 concave, waxy, pink petals about ¼" long and 10 conspicuous stamens.
Type locality: Lion Lake Trail, Canyon Creek, Swift Creek

216. SNOW-PLANT
Sarcodes sanguinea
Habitat: thick forest humus

WINTERGREEN FAMILY
Pyrolaceae
June

This is a thick fleshy saprophyte, brilliant red in color, which emerges following the melting snow. It is 1"-2" thick and 6"-12" tall and has scale-like leaves and bell-shaped flowers when fully developed.
Type locality: Lake Eleanor

217. SUGAR STICK
Allotropa virgata
Habitat: thick humus

WINTERGREEN FAMILY
Pyrolaceae
August

This is a saprophyte that lives on decaying organic matter in the soil. It is 5"-13" tall and is conspicuously striped with red and white like a candy-stick. The leaves are reduced to loose scales. The most conspicuous part of the flower is a crown-like circle of 10 blunt short stamens. There are no petals.
Type locality: Scott Mountain

218. RED COLUMBINE
Aguilegia formosa
Habitat: streambanks and damp woods

BUTTERCUP FAMILY
Ranunculaceae
July

Erect branching stems 1'-3' tall bear several drooping showy flowers. The hollow scarlet spurs ½"-¾" long that extend backward like 5 trumpets or horns make this plant distinctive. The forward portion of the petal is yellow. Spreading widely between the spurs are the sepals that are also scarlet. The leaves are deeply cleft, then variously lobed, and are chiefly basal.
Type locality: Sunrise Pass, Horse Haven Meadow, Deer Lake

219. RED LARKSPUR
Delphinium nudicaule
Habitat: dry brush covered slopes, lower elevations

BUTTERCUP FAMILY
Ranunculaceae
May

A hollow tubular cornucopia-shaped spur formed from the upper petal distinguishes the larkspurs. The spur of this species is nearly ¾" long and extends backwards horizontally. The flowers are a dull red with a touch of yellow. They form a loose cluster at the top of a nearly leafless stem 1'-2' long. The leaves are mostly basal and round in outline but deeply cleft into broad segments that in turn are shallowly lobed.
Type locality: Weaver Bally, Canyon Creek

220. DOUGLAS SPIRAEA   ROSE FAMILY
Spiraea douglasii   *Rosaceae*
Habitat: streambanks, moist places   July-August

This is an erect shrub 2'-4' high with reddish-brown stems. The leaves
are elliptic and coarsely toothed above the middle, 1"-2½" long. Tiny
soft pink flowers are crowded into terminal pyramid-shaped clusters 4"-
6" long. The stamens are excerted beyond the petals giving the flowers
a soft hairy appearance.
Type locality: Big Flat, Lion Lake Trail, Horse Haven Meadow

221. CALIFORNIA PITCHER PLANT   PITCHER PLANT FAMILY
(flower)
Darlingtonia californica   *Sarraceniaceae*
Habitat: marshy meadows and bogs   June-August

This is an insectivorous plant with greenish-yellow hollow leaves that
are hooded and have wing-like appendages resembling a fish-tail at the
mouth of the opening. (See #222.) The flowers are solitary and nodding
at the end of a tall, leafless stalk that is much longer than the leaves.
There are 5 yellow-green drooping sepals 1½"-2" long and 5 shorter
dark reddish-purple petals. Translucent spots in the dome of the leaves
and nectar secreted at the opening attract insects which become trapped
in the hollow leaves and are gradually digested by the plant.
Type locality: Swift Creek, Lake Eleanor, Echo Lake

222. CALIFORNIA PITCHER PLANT   PITCHER PLANT FAMILY
(leaves)
Darlingtonia californica   *Sarraceniaceae*
For description see #221.

223. MOUNTAIN SPIRAEA   ROSE FAMILY
Spiraea densiflora   *Rosaceae*
Habitat: rocky moist soil   July

This is a low, many stemmed, compact shrub 1'-3' high. Its opposite
leaves are elliptic, unevenly toothed, and about 1" long. The tiny, dainty
pink or rose colored flowers are crowded together in a dense, round-
topped cluster. The numerous stamens are longer than the petals giving
the cluster a soft appearance.
Type locality: Landers Lake, Deer Creek, Long Canyon

224. LAYNE'S MONKEY-FLOWER
Mimulus layneae
Habitat: dry sandy and gravelly places

FIGWORT FAMILY
Scrophulareaceae
July

There are over 75 species of mimulus in California. They are difficult to differentiate as minute details separate the species. This small mimulus is from 2"-8" tall. The rose to rose-violet flowers have a dark purple midrib in the center of each lobe with light ridges on the lower lobes. The leaves are elliptic, tapering to each end, up to 1" long, and somewhat sticky. A similar diminutive mimulus grows at lower elevations (*Mimulus kelloggii*). It has a crimson funnel-like flower with a long slender tube that has a yellow spot on the lower throat and is purple on the upper throat.
Type locality, *M. layneae*: Sapphire Lake
Type Locality, *M. kelloggii*: East Fork of East Weaver

225. SIERRA GOOSEBERRY
Ribes roezlii
Habitat: dry woods, open slopes

SAXIFRAGE FAMILY
Saxifragaceae
April-June

The gooseberries are distinguished by their conspicuous spines at the leaf nodes. This gooseberry is a stout shrub with leaves 1" long that are rounded and lobed. The flowers are pendulous and grow singly or in twos at the ends of short lateral branchlets. The dark red sepals are strongly reflexed when mature. The whitish petals are about half as long as the sepals and grow straight down resembling a white petticoat beneath a red velvet skirt.
Type locality: Union Creek, Big Flat, Wildwood

226. LITTLE ELEPHANT'S HEAD
Pedicularis attolens
Habitat: damp meadows

FIGWORT FAMILY
Scrophulareaceae
July

The small flowers of this plant are said to resemble the head, flapping ears, and trunk of an elephant. The flowers are in a compact elongated spike-like cluster at the end of an erect, somewhat leafless stem 6"-16" tall. The flowers are pink or pale lavender with dark lines and with a lighter area at the base of the lower petals. The upper petals are recurved and narrowed into an upcurved beak. The leaves are primarily basal and are finely divided into narrow segments.
Type locality: Black Basin, Diamond Lake, Deer Creek Meadow

227. MOUNTAIN PRIDE — FIGWORT FAMILY

227. MOUNTAIN PRIDE   FIGWORT FAMILY
Penstemon newberryi ssp. *berryi*   *Scrophulareaceae*
Habitat: open dry rocky slopes and crevices   July

This plant has numerous stems about 1' high that bear short one-sided clusters of crimson flowers 1"-1¼" long. The tubular flowers have a very short upper lip that is white bearded. The leathery leaves are elliptic, finely toothed, and about ¾" long.
Type locality: Caribou Basin, Coffee Creek, South Fork Mt.

228. LEWIS MONKEY-FLOWER   FIGWORT FAMILY
Mimulus lewisii   *Scrophulareaceae*
Habitat: streambanks, high elevations   August

The showy trumpet-like flowers of this mimulus are nearly 2" long with 5 spreading lobes. There are 2 light colored hairy ridges in the throat. The stems are simple and erect, 1'-2' tall, and have opposite sticky leaves 1"-2½" long.
Type locality: Kidd Creek Meadow, Canyon Creek

229. INDIAN WARRIOR   FIGWORT FAMILY
Pedicularis densiflora   *Scrophulareaceae*
Habitat: dry open woods   April-May

This plant might easily be mistaken for an Indian paint-brush. Minute botanical differences in the stamens and pistils place it in a different genus. The Indian warrior has compact clusters of dull red flowers at the ends of erect stems under 12" tall. The leaves, which are mostly basal, are a bronze-green color and are finely dissected into fern-like segments.
Type locality: Lion Lake Trail, Weaver Bally, Wildwood

230. WAVY-LEAVED INDIAN PAINT-BRUSH FIGWORT FAMILY
Castilleja applegatei   *Scrophulareaceae*
Habitat: dry places   July-August

This paint-brush is usually smaller than the great red Indian paint-brush (see #232). It rarely reaches 1½' tall. The herbage is somewhat hairy and sticky. The leaves have a wavy margin and are frequently lobed into irregular segments. The flowers vary from a scarlet to an orange-red touched with yellow.
Type locality: Horse Haven Meadow, Weaver Bally, Lake Eleanor

231. COPELAND'S OWL'S CLOVER
Orthocarpus copelandii
Habitat: open places

FIGWORT FAMILY
Scrophulareaceae
July-August

The owl's clover bears some similarity to the paint-brushes but it differs in that the white lower lip of the owl's clover is inflated and visible whereas with the paint-brush the flower parts are inconspicuous and dominated by long, usually bright red bracts. This plant has pink bracts ⅓" long, rose-purple petals, and an inflated white lower lip. It has opposite leaves that are slender and pointed, 1"-2" long. The simple erect stem is 4"-14" tall.
Type locality: Luella Lake, Deadfall Lake, Horse Haven Meadow

232. GREAT RED INDIAN PAINT-BRUSH
Castilleja miniata
Habitat: damp slopes and meadows

FIGWORT FAMILY
Scrophulareaceae
July-August

This paint-brush often grows taller than our other paint-brushes. The stems are smooth and erect, 2'-3' tall. The leaves are small, narrow or elliptic, and rarely lobed. The flowers are congested in a compact spike with many brilliantly colored deep red bracts and inconspicuous greenish-red petals.
Type locality: Black Basin, Lake Anna, Diamond Lake

233. NARROW-LEAVED MILKWEED
Asclepias fasicularis
Habitat: dry places

MILKWEED FAMILY
Asclepiadaceae
June

The limber stems of this species are usually 2' tall with wiry, narrow opposite leaves 5" long and ¼" wide. Roundish clusters of small greenish-white to lavender flowers grow in the axils of the leaves. Each flower has 5 strongly reflexed lobes and in the center a "crown-like" column surrounds the stamens. As with all milkweeds, a milky juice exudes freely from any cut or break in the plant.
Type locality: Weaverville

234. OOKOW
Brodiaea congesta
Habitat: dry grassy slopes

AMARYLLIS FAMILY
Amaryllidaceae
June

The blue-violet flowers of this brodiaea are borne in compact heads at the ends of naked stems up to 2' or 3' long. The individual flowers are about ¾" long and are somewhat constricted in the middle. There are 3

fertile stamens which helps distinguish it from a similar species with which it is sometimes confused. (*Brodiaea pulchella* has 6 stamens.) Botanists have not agreed upon the correct scientific names for the brodiaeas.
Type locality: Norwegian Meadow

235. ELEGANT BRODIAEA
Brodiaea elegans
Habitat: dry slopes and grassy areas

AMARYLLIS FAMILY
Amarylladaceae
June

This brodiaea has an erect sturdy stem 4"-16" tall that bears a loose cluster of funnel-shaped flowers. The stems of the individual flowers are ½"-3" long and all originate from the same point at the tip of the stem. The deep blue-purple flowers are 1"-1½" long and have spreading lobes. The leaves are narrow and usually have withered by the time the blossoms open.
Type locality: Weaverville

236. HARVEST BRODIAEA
Brodiaea coronaria
Habitat: dry meadows

AMARYLLIS FAMILY
Amaryllidaceae
June

Only minute differences separate this brodiaea from another brodiaea found in the area (see #235). Size is one factor. The flowers of this species are shorter (about 1" long) and the flower tube has a more rounded base. The flowers are also apt to be a lighter lilac-violet color. The flower clusters of both of these brodiaeas are a loose umbel.
Type locality: Norwegian Meadow

237. CASCADE OREGON GRAPE
Berberis nervosa
Habitat: coniferous woods

BARBERRY FAMILY
Berberidaceae
May-June

A single erect stem 12" tall covered with many brown awl-shaped scales distinguishes this barberry. The stem is terminated by a tuft of long, glossy evergreen leaves that are divided into several pairs of spiny-toothed leaflets 1½"-3" long. Yellow flowers stand erect from a terminal bud in dense elongated clusters.
Type locality: Hatchet Creek, Boulder Creek

238. HOUND'S TONGUE — BORAGE FAMILY
Cynoglossum grande — *Boraginaceae*
Habitat: open woods — May

The name of this plant is in reference to the shape of the leaves that are large and pointed, on petioles equally as long. The flowers are in a loose terminal cluster at the end of a nearly leafless stem up to 2' high. The petals are a clear bright blue, ½" long, and have at their throat a circle of white, bead-like crests.
Type locality: Musser Hill, French Creek, North Fork Trinity River

239. JESSICA'S STICKSEED — BORAGE FAMILY
Hackelia jessicae — *Boraginaceae*
Habitat: damp places — July

The flowers, resembling old-fashioned forget-me-nots, vary in color from blue to pink. They grow in loosely branched terminal clusters on stems 1½'-3' tall. There are 5 floral lobes about ¼" long with a conspicuous crest at their center. The leaves are long and narrow, are well distributed, and diminish in size along the stem. Its name comes from its fruit which readily sticks to clothing.
Type locality: Dorleska Mine, Kidd Creek, Long Canyon

240. WILKIN'S HAREBELL — BELL-FLOWER FAMILY
Campanula wilkinsiana — *Campanulaceae*
Habitat: streambanks, damp meadows — August

These bright blue flowers usually grow singly at the ends of simple erect stems about 6" long. The flower is bell-shaped, ½" long, and cut into 5 spreading pointed lobes. The stems are leafy and grow close together from a spreading rootstalk. It is one of our rare species and should be protected.
Type locality: Kidd Creek Meadows

241. CASCADE DOWINGEA — BELL-FLOWER FAMILY
Dowingea yina — *Campanulaceae*
Habitat: boggy places, vernal pools — July-August

The wide 3-lobed lower lip of the deep blue flowers of this low annual has a central yellow area bordered with white. The 2 lobes of the upper lip are considerably smaller and stand erect. The plant is from 2"-4" tall and has simple leaves that are narrow, ⅓" long, and well distributed along the stem.
Type locality: Big Flat, Packer Meadow

242. CALIFORNIA HAREBELL   BELL-FLOWER FAMILY
Campanula prenanthoides   *Campanulaceae*
Habitat: dry wooded areas   July-August

This plant has slender erect stems 1'-2' long. Most of the leaves are borne on the lower half of the stem. Along the upper half of the stem are scattered clusters of airy and fragile clear blue flowers. The slender petals are usually curled strongly back and are spread wide apart. A conspicuous pistil with its tip divided into 3 curved lobes extends well beyond the recurved petals.
Type locality: Big Flat, Stuarts Fork, Boulder Creek

243. CHICORY   SUNFLOWER FAMILY
Cichorium intybus   *Compositae*
Habitat: waste places   June

Clear light blue flowers are scattered along the naked stems of this branching composite that often reaches 5' in height. The flower heads sit closely against the stems and consist only of ray flowers, there being no center disc flowers. The rays are nearly 1" long and notched at the tips. The basal leaves are long and narrow, usually incised, and up to 8" long.
Type locality: Weaverville

244. SPREADING FLEABANE   SUNFLOWER FAMILY
Erigeron divergens   *Compositae*
Habitat: dry flats and slopes   July

The fleabanes are similar to asters but usually the flowers are small, flat, and have numerous narrow ray flowers. They bloom earlier in the summer than do the asters which generally are a late summer or fall flower. With the fleabanes the bracts beneath the flower head are all the same length. The branched stems of this species are 4"-12" long and bear many small, narrow leaves, ½"-1½" long. The numerous and very narrow ray flowers are ¼"-½" long and are usually a light blue color. The color, however, may also vary from white to a pale pink or lavender.
Type locality: Big Flat

245. WESTERN MOUNTAIN ASTER SUNFLOWER FAMILY

Aster occidentalis   *Compositae*
Habitat: moist or dry open places   August

The narrow leaves of this aster are 4" long at the base of the plant and gradually become smaller up the stem. The margins of the leaves are noticeably rough to the touch. The flower heads are from 1"-1¼" across and occur in rather close, nearly naked clusters. They have from 20-30 blue rays and a center of yellow disc flowers.
Type locality: Tangleblue Lake

246. CASCADE ASTER SUNFLOWER FAMILY

Aster ledophyllus   *Compositae*
Habitat: dry open rocky slopes   August

This aster stands 2' tall. The leaves are quite uniform in shape, 1¼"-2½" long and ¼"-¾" wide, and are numerous on the stems. The flower heads have from 6-15 violet rays which gives the flower cluster a very open, airy, and sometimes ragged appearance.
Type locality: Dorleska Mine, Kidd Creek

247. ALPINE ASTER SUNFLOWER FAMILY

Aster alpigenous ssp. *andersonii*   *Compositae*
Habitat: wet meadows   July-August

The grass-like leaves of this species help identify this aster. They grow in tufts and are up to 10" long and ½" wide. The stems, which are essentially leafless, are 6"-12" long and wooly toward the upper end. The stems bear a single showy flower head at the tip. The rays are lavender and about ½" long. The center disc flowers are yellow.
Type locality: Big Boulder Lake

248. BLUE-VEINED NEMOPHILA PHACELIA FAMILY

Nemophila menziesii var. *intermedia*   *Hydrophyllaceae*
Habitat: moist slopes   April

This plant has weak stems 4"-12" long. Its leaves are soft, opposite, 1"-2" long, and divided into many lobes or narrow segments. The pretty flowers, which stand well above the leaves, are bowl-shaped and 1" or more broad. They are pale blue to white with conspicuous blue veins. This is a variety of an extremely variable species which has blue petals and a pale center known as baby blue-eyes.
Type locality: Canyon Creek

249. MOUNTAIN SHIELDLEAF
Streptanthus tortuosus
Habitat: dry rocky slopes

MUSTARD FAMILY
Cruciferae
July

The leaves that clothe the stems of this plant are more distinctive than its flowers. They are concave, clasping, round or shield-shaped, 1"-3" broad. The flask-shaped flowers, ½" long, are borne in elongated clusters and have 4 small pale petals and sepals that are usually a purplish color. A variety, *Streptanthus tortuosus* var. *pallidus*, has yellowish sepals and petals veined with purple. It has been observed on Buckhorn Mountain.
Type locality: Lake Anna

250. YERBA SANTA
Eriodictyon californicum
Habitat: dry rocky slopes, mostly lower elevations

WATERLEAF FAMILY
Hydrophyllaceae
May

This woody plant is erect, loosely branched, and usually 3'-4' tall. It has brownish-green leaves that are thick and sticky. These leaves are long and narrow, tapered to both ends, markedly toothed on the margins, and have a network of conspicuous veins. The bluish-lavender flowers are funnel-like, ¼"-½" long, and occur in loosely coiled clusters.
Type locality: Weaverville

251. SQUAW LETTUCE
or CALIFORNIA WATERLEAF
Hydrophyllum occidentale
Habitat: open woods

PHACELIA FAMILY

Hydrophyllaceae
May-June

Commonly growing less than 1' high, it is the leaves of this plant that are most readily noticed. They are about 6" long, roughly hairy, and divided into several oblong segments or divisions. The white to pale lavender flowers grow in compact terminal clusters. The petals are about ⅓" long with protruding stamens and pistils which give the flower a fuzzy appearance.
Type locality: Backbone Creek, Horse Haven Meadows

252. DRAPERIA
Draperia systyla
Habitat: dry slopes in woods

PHACELIA FAMILY
Hydrophyllaceae
July

This low herb usually has several stems 4"-6" long. Its simple opposite leaves are 1"-2" long and covered with silky hairs. The flowers are pale violet, funnel-form in shape, ½" long, and crowded in terminal branched clusters.
Type locality: Stuarts Fork

253. SPOTTED FRITILLARY
Fritillaria glauca
Habitat: dry serpentine slopes

LILY FAMILY
Liliaceae
April-May

The simple stems of this plant are from 3"-7" tall and bear nodding flowers that are mottled with shades of yellow and purplish-brown. The flowers have 6 straight (not reflexed) petal-like segments ¾" long and ¼" wide. There are 2-4 slender alternate leaves 2"-4" long.
Type locality: Musser Hill

254. BLUE-EYED GRASS
Sisyrinchium bellum
Habitat: moist grassy areas

IRIS FAMILY
Iridaceae
June-July

This tufted member of the iris family is grass-like in appearance. It has narrow leaves usually shorter than the flattened flowering stem. The 3-7 purplish-blue flowers growing at the tip of the stem have darker veins on each of the 6 flower segments and a spot of yellow at the base. Each segment is about ½" long and has a short bristle at the tip. It grows to a height of about 10"-16".
Type locality: Mumford Meadows, Big Flat

255. GREEN GENTIAN
Frasera albicaulis ssp. *nitida*
Habitat: dry or gravelly slopes

GENTIAN FAMILY
Gentianaceae
June

The slender erect stems of this gentian are 10"-18" tall and have long narrow opposite leaves that have a distinctive white marking along the margins. The flowers are whitish to bluish with purple dots inside and a greenish gland in the center of each lobe. There are 4 pointed floral lobes, ⅓" long, that spread wide horizontally. The 4 stamens attached to the lobes stand almost erect. The flowers grow in whorls in an irregular pattern along the upper 6" of the stem.
Type locality: Norwegian Meadows, Lake Eleanor

256. BLUE GENTIAN
Gentiana calycosa
Habitat: meadows and streambanks

GENTIAN FAMILY
Gentianaceae
August

This plant blooms late in the summer and has a deep blue, bell-shaped flower marked with a tinge of green in the throat. Flowers occur singly or in pairs at the tips of the straight stems that are 6"-12" high. The flower is about 1" long with erect rounded lobes ¼" long. Between the

lobes are 2 small pointed appendages. The several stems grow in a tufted group and bear several pairs of opposite oval leaves 1" long.
Type locality: Mumford Meadows, Lois Lake

257. MOUNTAIN PENNYROYAL   MINT FAMILY
Monardella odoratissima ssp. *glauca*   *Labiatae*
Habitat: dry slopes, open ridges   July

This is similar to the more common pale pennyroyal but the stems and the herbage have a reddish-purple cast (see #258). The flower heads are more globose and have bracts that are often deep rose-purple in color subtended by 2 other bracts that are green and leaf-like.
Type locality: Sunrise Pass, Fox Lake

258. PALE PENNYROYAL   MINT FAMILY
Monardella odoratissima ssp. *pallida*   *Labiatae*
Habitat: dry slopes   July-August

This pennyroyal usually grows in clumps. It has square stems, light ash in color, up to 1' tall and has light green opposite leaves that are somewhat oval, narrowing at the apex and up to 1¼" long. The pale lavender flowers are crowded into flat-topped heads about 1" in diameter.
Type locality: Deer Creek Meadows, Luella Lake, Weaver Bally

259. WESTERN BLUE FLAX   FLAX FAMILY
Linum perenne ssp. *lewisii*   *Linaceae*
Habitat: dry slopes and ridges, higher elevations   June-July

This flax usually has several very slender and weak stems from ½'-2½' tall. The leaves are thickly distributed along the stem. There are several clear blue flowers ½"-1" long in a loose cluster at the ends of the stems. The petals are delicate and tend to drop easily.
Type locality: Luella Lake, Deadfall Lakes

260. HEDGE-NETTLE   MINT FAMILY
Stachys rigida   *Labiatae*
Habitat: moist places   July

This plant is covered with stiff hairs and has square stems 2'-4' tall. The opposite oblong leaves, 1½"-4" long, are wider at the base, taper to a point, and have a toothed margin. The flowers are pale lavender and sometimes veined with purple. They are strongly 2-lipped and occur in long terminal spikes.
Type locality: Horse Haven Meadow

261. SELF-HEAL — MINT FAMILY

Prunella vulgaris ssp. *lanceolata* — *Labiatae*
Habitat: moist woods — June-July

This is a low herb with square stems and opposite leaves that are narrowly oval, pointed at the tip, and 1"-2" long. The flowers are mostly violet, about ½" long, and grow in dense terminal spikes. They are 2-lipped with the upper lip erect and arched and the lower lip divided into 3 lobes, the center lobe being somewhat toothed or fringed.
Type locality: Norwegian Meadow, Horse Haven Meadow

262. CREEPING SAGE — MINT FAMILY

Salvia sonomensis — *Labiatae*
Habitat: dry slopes — May

This member of the mint family has creeping, leafy, somewhat matted stems and erect leafless flower stalks up to 16" long. There is a terminal cluster of 4-6 dense whorls of bluish flowers that are tubular in form and about ½" long. The flowers are 2-lipped with an upper lip that is short and erect and a lower lip that is much longer. The leaves are basal and over 2" long. As with all mints the stems are square.
Type locality: Musser Hill

263. AMERICAN VETCH — PEA FAMILY

Vicia americana var. *oregana* — *Leguminoseae*
Habitat: open places — June

The vetches are trailing plants that support their stems by means of tendrils. This vetch has 4-8 pairs of leaflets on short zigzag stems. Grouped at the end of a naked flower stalk are 3-6 purplish pea-like flowers ½"-¾" long.
Type locality: Norwegian Meadow

264. SNAPDRAGON SKULLCAP — MINT FAMILY

Scutellaria antirrhinoides — *Labiatae*
Habitat: dry slopes — July

This plant looks more like a snapdragon than a mint. The flowers are borne in the axils of opposite leaves although they twist so as to appear to be on one side of the stem. The stems are square and about 10" long. The dark blue flowers, ½"-¾" long, have an upper lip that is arched like a helmet and a lower lip that is 3-lobed.
Type locality: Horse Haven Meadows, Yellow Rose Mine Trail, Long Canyon

265. LYALL'S LUPINE
Lupinus lyallii
Habitat: dry gravelly slopes, high elevations

PEA FAMILY
Leguminoseae
July-August

This is a short stubby lupine barely 4" tall. The flowers are purple, ⅓" long, and crowded into compact head-like clusters rather than in elongated spikes. The palmate leaves have leaflets about ½" long. The entire plant is covered with silky hairs.
Type locality: Head of North Fork of Coffee Creek

266. BROAD-LEAVED LUPINE
Lupinos latifolius
Habitat: open places

PEA FAMILY
Leguminoseae
August

There are over 80 species of lupines in California. They are extremely variable and difficult to identify without close examination for minute botanical differences. As a group they will have palmate leaves with several leaflets emerging from a common point in a very precise pattern. The flowers are all pea-like and grow in spike-like elongated terminal clusters. The color is usually bluish but there are some species that are whitish, reddish, or yellowish. The blue flowers of this lupine are ¼"-⅓" long in a very elongated flower cluster. Its leaves have 7-9 broad leaflets, 1½"-4" long which are widest at the tip.
Type locality: Kidd Creek

267. SICKLE-KEELED LUPINE
Lupinus albicaulis
Habitat: open area, higher elevations

PEA FAMILY
Leguminoseae
June-July

The stems of this lupine are erect, often branched, and about 2' tall with leaves well distributed along the stem. The flowers, which are whitish to bluish fading to brown, grow in a cluster up to 12" long and tend to be slender.
Type locality: Horse Haven Bench

268. CAMAS
Camassis quamash
Habitat: wet meadows

LILY FAMILY
Liliaceae
May

Camas often grows in large colonies transforming a wet meadow into a "sea of blue". Its stout flowering stem, about 2' high, bears an elongated terminal cluster of numerous deep blue-violet flowers. There are 3 petals and 3 petal-like sepals of similar size and color making the flower appear star-shape. There are 6 conspicuous stamens that are also widely

spreading. A second very similar species (*Camas leichtinii*) which occurs inland is somewhat larger and differs but slightly from the coastal species.
Type locality: Hetten Valley

269. STAR TULIP   LILY FAMILY
Calochortus nudus   *Liliaceae*
Habitat: damp ground   June-July

This bowl-shaped "tulip-like" flower has 3 broad, rounded lavender petals about ¾" long. A single flower grows at the end of a naked stem 4"-10" tall. There is a solitary basal leaf ½" wide, shorter than the flower stem.
Type locality: Union Lake, Luella Lake, Norwegian Meadow

270. NAKED BROOM-RAPE   BROOM-RAPE FAMILY
Orobanche uniflora var. *purpurea*   *Orobanchaceae*
Habitat: open places   April

This is a parasitic herb which gets its nourishment from the roots of other plants. The stem is mostly underground. A single blue-purple flower having a spot of yellow in a somewhat constricted throat grows at the tip of a naked flower stalk 2"-6" tall.
Type locality: Weaver Bally

271. SQUAW CARPET   BUCKTHORN FAMILY
Ceanothus prostratus   *Rhamnaceae*
Habitat: wooded slopes   June

This is a trailing shrub which forms a dense ground cover. The opposite leaves are thick, leathery, prickly to the touch, holly-like in appearance, and about 1" long. The tiny flowers vary in color from a light blue to a bright blue and grow in small loose globose clusters.
Type locality: Weaver Bally

272. DWARF CEANOTHUS   BUCKTHORN FAMILY
Ceanothus pumilus   *Rhmanaceae*
Habitat: dry serpentine slopes   May

This is a low spreading shrub with rigid reddish branches and leathery leaves ¼"-1" long. There are usually 3 holly-like teeth on the margins of each side of the leaf. The flowers are a bright blue and grow in tight globose clusters about ¾" across.
Type locality: North Fork Trinity River Trail

273. BLUE FIELD GILIA   PHLOX FAMILY
Gilia capitata   *Polemoneaceae*
Habitat: dry rocky slopes, open woods   July

Dense globose heads of small pale blue flowers grow at the ends of loosely branched slender stems 1'-2' or more tall. The leaves are mostly basal or sparsely scattered along the lower half of the stem. They are ½"-1¼" long and twice divided into small narrow segments.
Type locality: Caribou Trail, Buckhorn Mt.

274. DWARF LARKSPUR   BUTTERCUP FAMILY
Delphinium nuttallianum   *Ranunculaceae*
Habitat: rocky meadows and slopes   July

The slender stems of this larkspur are 6"-18" tall and have rounded leaves 1"-2" in diameter that are palmately divided into narrow segments. The flowers are deep blue with a touch of white on the upper petal. The spur is about ½" long. There may be but a few or there may be many blossoms in the loose flower cluster.
Type locality: Bear Basin, Rush Creek

275. DEER BRUSH   BUCKTHORN FAMILY
Ceanothus integerrimus   *Rhamnaceae*
Habitat: open wooded slopes   June

This is a loosely branched shrub that is usually about 4' tall but can grow considerably taller. In contrast with many of the other species of ceanothus that have rigid stems and coarse leaves the smaller branches and leaves of this shrub are flexible. Its oval leaves are about 2" long and make succulent deer feed. The color of the small flowers is variable but most often is a pale blue. The flower clusters are long and tapering, 3"-4" or more in length and 1"-3" wide.
Type locality: Long Canyon Trail, Weaver Bally, Trinity Center

276. LEMMON'S CEANOTHUS   BUCKTHORN FAMILY
Ceanothus lemmonii   *Rhamnaceae*
Habitat: open slopes, lower elevations   May

This is a spreading shrub under 3' tall with gray to whitish bark. The leaves are oblong to rounded tapering to the base. The plant blooms profusely and makes a showy display. The bright blue flowers are tiny and form small rounded clusters ½"-1¼" long.
Type locality: Rush Creek, Weaverville

277. TALL MOUNTAIN LARKSPUR — BUTTERCUP FAMILY

Delphinium glaucum — *Ranunculaceae*
Habitat: wet meadows or streamsides — July-August

The flowers of the larkspur are characterized by the upper sepal which forms a backward spur resembling a dunce cap. The various species are difficult to distinguish from each other. This species is a stout plant growing 3'-5' tall. It has large rounded leaves about 6" in diameter that are divided into 5-7 broad segments. The dark blue-purple flower has a spur abut 3/8" long. The elongated flower cluster covers the upper 4"-16" of the stem.
Type locality: Horse Haven Meadow, Dorleska Mine, Deer Creek

278. MONKSHOOD — BUTTERCUP FAMILY

Aconitum columbianum — *Ranunculaceae*
Habitat: moist meadows or along streams — July-August

With this plant the upper sepal is arched to form a cap that looks like a monk's hood or a friar's cap. This is an erect plant 3'-4' tall. The leaves are 2"-4" across and deeply cleft into 3-5 divisions which are again divided into narrow segments. The flowers are usually a deep blue but occasionally white ones will be seen.
Type locality: Horse Haven Meadow, Long Canyon, Kidd Creek

279. BLUE PENSTEMON or GAY PENSTEMON — FIGWORT FAMILY

Penstemon laetus ssp. *roezlii* — *Scrophulareaceae*
Habitat: dry rocky slopes — June-August

This is a bell-shaped or tubular 2-lipped flower, blue-violet in color and about 1" long. It has a wide or gaping throat. Numerous narrow leaves ½"-2" long crowd the lower part of the stems of which there are several up to 1½' long.
Type locality: Ramshorn Creek, Dorleska Mine Trail

280. TORREY'S BLUE-EYED MARY — FIGWORT FAMILY

Collinsia torreyi var. *latifolia* — *Scrophulareaceae*
Habitat: open sandy slopes — July

The collinsias are all herbaceous plants with opposite leaves and flowers that are usually blue or lavendar together with white. The flowers are 2-lipped, the upper lip being divided into 2 upright lobes and the lower lip having 3 lobes although the middle lobe is not readily apparent as it is

hidden beneath the other two. This species is up to 8" tall and has stems that are usually branched with leaves that are 3 or 4 times as long as they are wide. The flowers are about ¼" long. The upper 2 lobes stand erect and are creamy white with purple spots in the throat. The lower lip is longer, dark blue in color and bends downward. (See also #281, #282.)
Type locality: Dorleska Mine Trail, Alpine Lake

281. DELICATE BLUE-EYED MARY FIGWORT FAMILY
Collinsia linearis *Scrophulareaceae*
Habitat: open woods May-June

This delicate plant, 4"-8" tall, has flowers borne on thread-like stems up to ½" long. There are small slender bracts beneath the loose whorls of flowers. The flowers, which are ⅓"-½" long, have bluish lower lobes and upright upper lobes that are whitish and bent back slightly.
Type locality: Weaver Bally, Horse Haven Bench

282. LARGE-FLOWERED BLUE-EYED MARY FIGWORT FAMILY
Collinsia grandiflora var. *pusilla* *Scrophulareaceae*
Habitat: open grassy or rocky places May

This collinsia has an erect stem 6"-8" tall with 3-7 flowers growing in the axils of the opposite leaves giving the appearance of being a whorled cluster. See #280 for general description of the collinsias. In this variety the flowers are quite blue and nearly ½" long.
Type locality: Little French Creek

283. PARISH'S NIGHTSHADE POTATO FAMILY
Solanum parishii *Solanaceae*
Habitat: dry slopes May-June

The flattish, spreading, 5-angled flowers of the nightshade make it easy to recognize. The flowers are lavender, about ¾" across, and grow in loose clusters on slender, slightly angled stems. There are 5 conspicuous short stamens crowded together around the central pistil. The fruit is a small round berry.
Type locality: Weaverville, Preacher Meadow

284. VERONICA
or COPELAND'S SPEEDWELL
Veronica copelandii
Habitat: serpentine slopes, higher elevations

FIGWORT FAMILY
Scrophulareaceae
July

These are small plants with erect stems about 6" long bearing small clusters of deep blue flowers that have 4 rounded petals of unequal size, the upper petal being broader than the others. There are 2 long stamens and a conspicuous style nearly ¼" long. The leafy stems bear opposite sticky leaves ½" long that are oblong and pointed.
Type locality: Diamond Lake, Black Basin

285. WHORLED PENSTEMON
Penstemon procerus
Habitat: mountain slopes, higher elevations

FIGWORT FAMILY
Scrophulareaceae
July

The flowers of this penstemon are crowded in whorls on the upper part of short stems. The flowers are blue-purple, tubular, 2-lipped, and about ½" long. The leaves, which are mostly near the base, are narrow and sometimes folded.
Type locality: Canyon Creek

286. SMALL-FLOWERED PENSTEMON
Penstemon procerus ssp. *brachyanthus*
Habitat: open slopes

FIGWORT FAMILY
Scrophulareaceae
August

This penstemon grows in rather dense clumps and has erect stems up to 12" tall. The flowers are a rose-purple and grow in interrupted clusters on the slender stems. The narrow leaves are opposite and grow primarily on the lower half of the stem.
Type locality: Kidd Creek Basin

287. COMMON VERBENA
Verbena lasiostachys
Habitat: widespread, dry open areas

VERVAIN FAMILY
Verbenaceae
May-June

This branching herb grows to nearly 3' in height. It has coarsely toothed leaves 1"-2½" long and tiny violet-blue flowers. The flowers are tubular with 5 lobes about 1/8" long. Only a few flowers are open at one time on the long slender spikes that usually occur in threes at the end of the hairy stems.
Type locality: Norwegian Meadow, Weaverville

288. SISKIYOU PENSTEMON FIGWORT FAMILY
Penstemon anguineus *Scrophulareaceae*
Habitat: dry woods July-August

This penstemon is rather straggly with spreading stems up to 2½' long. The blue-purple flowers are tubular and 2-lipped, the 2 lobes of the upper lip being more or less erect and shorter than those of the lower lip. The flowers are ½"-¾" long and grow in elongated clusters along the upper 8" of the stem. The leaves are oval, about ½" long, diminishing in size up the stem.
Type locality: East Weaver Lake, Boulder Lake

289. BIG-LEAF MAPLE (leaves) MAPLE FAMILY
Acer marcophyllum *Aceraceae*
Habitat: streambanks and canyons below 5000' April-May

This is a broad-crowned tree which can reach a height of 90' but more commonly it is 30'-50' tall. Its large leaves set it apart from all other maples. They are deeply palmately cleft into 3-5 irregularly indented lobes and are 10" or more broad. In the autumn they turn a clear golden-yellow. The flowers are numerous, greenish-yellow in color, about 1/8" long, and grow in drooping clusters or racemes. They develop into conspicuous winged fruits. (See #290.)
Type locality: Coffee Creek, Rush Creek, Slate Creek

290. BIG-LEAF MAPLE (flower and fruit) MAPLE FAMILY
Acer marcophyllum *Aceraceae*
For description see #289.

291. MADRONE HEATH FAMILY
Arbutus menziesii *Ericaceae*
Habitat: foothills and mountain slopes, lower elevations April-May

The tall straight, often leaning, trunks of this tree are its most interesting feature. It has a very thin, smooth, reddish-brown bark except at the base of older trees where it becomes thick with small dark plate-like scales. During the heat of midsummer the thin bark dries, splits, peels back and falls away exposing a fresh pea-green bark beneath that, as it dries, gradually turns a rust color. In the spring it produces dense clusters of waxy white urn-shaped flowers, ¼" long, that develop into clusters of orange-red berries ⅓" in diameter. The leaves are persistent, leathery, elliptic, and 2"-4½" long. (See also #292.)
Type locality: Boulder Creek, Canyon Creek

292. MADRONE (bark)   HEATH FAMILY
Arbutus menziesii   *Ericaceae*
For description see #291.

293. MOUNTAIN DOGWOOD (fruit)   DOGWOOD FAMILY
Cornus nuttallii   *Cornaceae*
For description see #294.

294. MOUNTAIN DOGWOOD (flower)   DOGWOOD FAMILY
Cornus nuttallii   *Cornaceae*
Habitat: lower mountain slopes and canyons   May

This is a small tree 10'-30' tall with opposite long-oval leaves that are pointed at the tip, 2½"-4½" long and 1¼"-2¾" wide. The leaves are especially showy in the fall when they change to shades of pinks and reds. What appears to be the flower of this dogwood is, instead, a dense cluster of numerous tiny white flowers surrounded by 4-7 conspicuous white petal-like bracts 2" long. The small flowers develop into clusters of scarlet fruits. (See also #293.)
Type locality: Canyon Creek, Coffee Creek, Tannery Gulch

295. CREEK DOGWOOD   DOGWOOD FAMILY
Cornus californica   *Cornaceae*
Habitat: streambanks   June-July

This is a tall shrub 5'-15' high with opposite leaves 2"-4" long that are elliptical and taper to a pointed tip. The small creamy-white flowers have 4 petals 1/8" long and occur in compact, somewhat rounded clusters 2" broad. The small fruits are round and white, ¼" in diameter.
Type locality: Long Canyon, Granite Peak Trail

296. BLACK-FRUIT DOGWOOD   DOGWOOD FAMILY
Cornus sessilis   *Cornaceae*
Habitat: streambanks, low elevations   April

This is a shrub or small tree with leaves that are broadly elliptic and bluntly pointed, 3"-4" long. The flowers are very tiny and inconspicuous and grow in the axils of the leaves. They develop into shiny, egg-shaped fruits about ½" long that are at first a pale green, then yellow, red, and finally a shiny black.
Type locality: Tannery Gulch

297. CALIFORNIA BLACK OAK (leaves)   OAK FAMILY
Quercus kelloggii   *Fagaceae*
For description see #298.

298. CALIFORNIA BLACK OAK (trunk)   OAK FAMILY
Quercus kelloggii   *Fagaceae*
Habitat: mountain slopes

The black oak usually has long and straight, or sometimes leaning or arched, trunks. The lower 10'-20' of the trunk of mature trees are usually clear of branches giving the tree a broad rounded crown. This is in contrast to the Oregon white oak whose trunk and branching is usually more twisted or angular (see #299). The leaves are deeply cleft and have about 3 lobes on each side of the midrib. There are one or more prickles at the tip of each lobe (see #297). This also contrasts with the white oak which has leaves with smooth rounded lobes and no prickles (see #300). The acorn of this oak is 1"-1¼" long and sits in a deep cup ½" deep and over 1" broad.
Type locality: Boulder Creek, Stuarts Fork

299. OREGON WHITE OAK (tree)   OAK FAMILY
Quercus garryana   *Fagaceae*
Habitat: dry gravelly slopes, lower elevations

This oak is usually shorter than the black oak. Its stout, spreading branches often give it a gnarled appearance when full grown. The thick leaves have 3 smooth rounded lobes on each side which do not have the prickles at their tips that characterize the black oak. The acorns have a very shallow cup and a rounded nut about 1¼" long. A shrub form of this oak known as the Brewer oak (*Q. garryana* var. *breweri*) grows at higher elevations. Its leaves are only about 2" long whereas those of the species are from 4"-6" long.
Type locality, Oregon White Oak: Squirrel Flat, Weaver Bally
Type locality, Brewer Oak: Yellow Rose Mine Trail

300. BREWER OAK (leaves)   OAK FAMILY
Quercus garryana var. *breweri*   *Fagaceae*
For description see #299.

301. SHRUB TAN OAK   OAK FAMILY
or DWARF TANBARK OAK   *Fagaceae*
Lithocarpus densiflora var. *echinoides*   June
Habitat: dry slopes

This is a shrub form of the tanbark oak and grows to a height of about 10'. Its evergreen leathery leaves are oblong, rounded at both ends and 1"-3" long. This is an acorn bearing species but it differs from the oaks in that the cup of the acorn is burr-like and the staminate catkins stand erect rather than hang pendulous. The tree form of the tanbark oak which can reach a height of 125' is found in Trinity County on South Fork Mountain and at other scattered locations. The leaves of the tree are twice the size of those of the shrub or dwarf form.
Type locality: Boulder Creek

302. SADLER OAK   OAK FAMILY
Quercus sadleriana   *Fagaceae*
Habitat: dry slopes, middle elevations

This is a shrub with many stems 3'-8' tall and with leaves that are more chestnut-like than oak-like. They are elliptical to oblong, 3"-4½" long and 1"-2" wide, with prominent, evenly spaced, lateral veins. The acorn is about ¾" long with the cup enclosing at least ⅓ of the nut.
Type locality: Lake Eleanor, Boulder Creek

303. BUSH CHINQUAPIN   OAK FAMILY
Castanopsis sempervirens   *Fagaceae*
Habitat: dry slopes or ridges

This is a spreading shrub 1½'-8' tall often forming thickets. The leaves are narrowly oblong, 1"-3" long and ½"-1" wide. They are a yellowish-green or gray-green color above and a pale rusty color beneath. Instead of having an acorn cup as do the oaks the nut of the chinquapin is enclosed in a spiny bur.
Type locality: Boulder Creek

304. HUCKLEBERRY OAK   OAK FAMILY
Quercus vaccinifolia   *Fagaceae*
Habitat: mountain slopes, middle elevations

This is a small shrub but it is included in this section because of its relationship to the other oaks. It is a compact evergreen shrub from 1'-4' tall. It has many slender pliable branches and leaves that are oblong,

often pointed at the tip, ½"-1¼" long and about ½" wide. They are dull green in color and have a smooth edge. The acorn is about ½" long with a shallow cup that is ½" wide and covered with a whitish wooly coating.
Type locality: Boulder Creek, Swift Creek

305. CALIFORNIA BUCKEYE

BUCKEYE FAMILY

Aesculus californica
Habitat: dry slopes, lower elevations

Hippocastanaceae
June

This is a broad bush or small tree up to 20' tall with opposite leaves that are palmately divided into 5-7 narrow leaflets 3"-6" long. Small white or pinkish flowers grow in erect cylindrical clusters. The fruits are pear-shaped, 2"-3" long, and hang conspicuously from the ends of the branches.
Type locality: Rush Creek

306. QUAKING ASPEN

WILLOW FAMILY

Populus tremuloides
Habitat: damp and open slopes or flats, higher elevations

Salicaceae

The smooth, greenish-white bark of the quaking aspen makes this tree easy to recognize. Its maximum height is about 40' but when it grows in thickets it has an irregular and crooked trunk and branches. The leaves are almost round with a short point at the tip giving them a somewhat triangular shape. There is a slender petiole 1½"-3" long that is flattened at right angles to the leaf blade causing the leaves to tremble with the slightest breeze.
Type locality: Stuarts Fork, Big Flat

307. MOUNTAIN ASH (fruit)

ROSE FAMILY

Sorbus scopulina
Habitat: streambanks and canyon bottoms

Rosaceae
July

This is a tall, many-stemmed shrub 9' high with leaves that are pinnately divided into 7-15 finely toothed leaflets. Numerous small white flowers grow in flat-topped clusters 2"-3" across. The species is most readily recognized by its distinctive small coral-red berry-like fruit which develop in the late summer.
Type locality: Papoose Lake, Canyon Creek

308. BITTER CHERRY (flowers)   ROSE FAMILY
Prunus emarginata   *Rosaceae*
Habitat: open brush fields and ridges   May

Often forming thickets, this loosely branching shrub has long slender branches that are usually reddish in color. The leaves are oblong, finely toothed and 1"-1½" long. Its small white flowers, ½" across, are grouped in short rounded clusters. Its fruits are clear red, about ¼" in diameter, and very bitter.
Type locality: Long Gulch Trail, Bear Lake Trail, Weaver Bally

309. HAZELNUT (staminate flower)   BIRCH FAMILY
Corylus rostrata var. *californica*   *Betulaceae*
Habitat: moist slopes and canyons   April

This open, spreading shrub reaches 10' in height. Its leaves are somewhat oval, doubly toothed, often velvety, 1½"-3" long. There are separate staminate and pistillate flowers. The staminate (with stamens) are drooping catkins. The pistillate (with pistils) are small rounded buds with the long red stigmas of the pistils protruding from them. The fruit is a nut which is enveloped by fuzzy bracts that are often elongated into a fringed tip. The hazelnut is related to the filbert nuts of the commercial trade. (See also #310.)
Type locality: Stuarts Fork, East Weaver Creek

310. HAZELNUT (pistillate flower)   BIRCH FAMILY
Corylus rostrata var. *californica*   *Betulaceae*
For description see #309.

311. BLACK COTTONWOOD   WILLOW FAMILY
Populus tricocarpa   *Salicaceae*
Habitat: stream banks and canyon bottoms

This cottonwood grows tall and straight. Its height can exceed 100'. The bark has cleanly channeled longitudinal fissures separating long narrow plates. Its leaves are somewhat oval, 3"-7" long, tapering to a point at the tip. The leaves are longer than they are wide. This distinguishes it from the Fremont cottonwood that has leaves that are wider than they are long and which also grows in the Trinity Mountains.
Type locality: Coffee Creek

312. WESTERN CHOKECHERRY — ROSE FAMILY
Prunus virginiana var. *demissa* — *Rosaceae*
Habitat: brushy slopes, moist places, lower elevations — May

This is an erect shrub 3'-12' tall. The simple oval leaves are very finely toothed, pointed at the tip, and 1½"-3½" long. Numerous small white flowers form elongated cylindrical clusters 2"-5" long. The fruits are round, dark red, about ¼" long, bitter but edible.
Type locality: Weaverville

313. PONDEROSA PINE (bark) — PINE FAMILY
Pinus ponderosa — *Pinaceae*
For description see #314.

314. PONDEROSA PINE (tree) — PINE FAMILY
Pinus ponderosa — *Pinaceae*
Habitat: dry slopes, lower elevations

This is a massive tree with a straight trunk that can reach 230' in height and 8' in diameter. It has short, often pendulous branches that turn up at the ends with brush-like tufts of foliage. The bark consists of large plates of yellowish to reddish-brown scales which bring to mind the pieces of a jigsaw puzzle. The needles are in a bundle of 3 and vary in length from 5"-11". They are yellow-green in color. Its cones are oval, 3"-6" in length, with spreading scales that have short prickles at the tips making the cone prickly to the touch when clasped.
Type locality: Stuarts Fork, Big Flat

315. JEFFREY PINE (needles) — PINE FAMILY
Pinus jeffreyi — *Pinaceae*
For description see #316.

316. JEFFREY PINE (tree) — PINE FAMILY
Pinus jeffreyi — *Pinaceae*
Habitat: dry slopes, middle elevations

The jeffrey pine is closely related to the ponderosa pine. Several similarities or differences can be noted. The bark of the jeffrey pine tends to be darker and redder than that of the ponderosa. A pleasant vanilla-like odor is detectable in its deep furrows, especially on a warm sunny day. The needles, in bundles of 3, are blue-green in color rather than the yellow-green of the ponderosa. The cones, which are 6"-10" in length, are larger than those of the ponderosa and are smooth to the touch when clasped. (See also #315.)
Type locality: Big Flat

317. SUGAR PINE
Pinus lambertiana
Habitat: mixed with other conifers, 2500'-5000' elevations

PINE FAMILY
Pinaceae

This is probably our most majestic pine. When full grown it has long side branches spreading out horizontally for great distances like huge arms. Its blue-green needles, in bundles of 5, are slender and sharp pointed. They are 1¾"-4" long, shorter and finer than those of the ponderosa pine with which it is sometimes associated. Its enormous, relatively slender cones are between 1' and 1½' long and hang in clusters from the ends of the upper branches. The bark on old trunks is deeply furrowed and irregularly divided into long thick plate-like ridges.
Type locality: Boulder Creek Trail, East Fork Coffee Creek, Rush Creek

318. WESTERN WHITE PINE
Pinus monticola
Habitat: elevations above 4500'

PINE FAMILY
Pinaceae

This pine is closely related to the sugar pine but grows at higher elevations. The needles are also in bundles of 5 and look very much like those of the sugar pine. The cones are the easiest way to identify this pine. They are much shorter than those of the sugar pine being only 4"-8" long. They have similar structure but their tendency to be slightly curved helps distinguish them from immature sugar pine cones. The bark of this species is broken into small rectangular plates. This contrasts with that of the sugar pine which is deeply fissured into long narrow ridges. (See #317.)
Type locality: Mirror Lake, Siligo Meadow, Dorleska Mine

319. FOXTAIL PINE
Pinus balfouriana
Habitat: rocky ridges and slopes above 5000'

PINE FAMILY
Pinaceae

This is a short tree that usually grows to a height of about 45'. It has short rigid spreading branches. On ridge tops there is often a wind-blown aspect to the tree. The needles, which are short and stiff, blue-green in color and persist on the branch for several years, are crowded into tufts at the ends of the branches for a distance of about 10"-20". This gives the branches a brush-like aspect which could possibly resemble the bushy tail of a fox. The cones of this pine are 4"-5" long and have scales with a similarity in form to those of the western white pine for it is also a 5 needle pine and therefore a member of the white pine group.
Type locality: Deer Creek, Summit Lake

320. FOXTAIL PINE (needles and cones)   PINE FAMILY
Pinus balfouriana   *Pinaceae*
For description see #319.

321. DIGGER PINE   PINE FAMILY
Pinus sabiniana   *Pinaceae*
Habitat: dry foothills, lower elevations

The gray-green color of the sparse foliage of the digger pine and the
long upright forks of the trunk with crooked and often drooping side
branches distinguishes this pine from others. The needles are in bundles
of 3, 8"-12" long and have a tendency to droop. The cones are heavy
and large, 6"-12" long with triangular spur-like hooks at the tips of the
cone scales. (See also #322.)
Type locality: Trinity River Canyon, Weaverville

322. DIGGER PINE (needles)   PINE FAMILY
Pinus sabiniana   *Pinaceae*
For description see #321.

323. LODGEPOLE PINE   PINE FAMILY
Pinus murrayana   *Pinaceae*
Habitat: dry slopes, middle elevations

This is a tree of variable form depending upon the density of the stand.
Ours are usually in open stands, therefore the trees are stocky, open and
much branched. They are usually about 50'-60' tall but occasionally
they grow considerably taller. The needles are thick, about 2" long, in
bundles of 2. The older needles become curved with age and remain on
the branch for several years. The cones are small, 1½"-2" long, with
rather thin scales that usually open when mature even though the cone
has persisted on the tree.
Type locality: Lilypad Lake, Horse Haven Meadows

324. YEW   YEW FAMILY
Taxus brevifolia   *Taxaceae*
Habitat: canyons and streambanks, 2000'-5000'

This is a small tree that occasionally reaches 75' but more commonly is
20'-30' tall. It has a broad open crown with slender spreading horizontal
branches and branchlets that often hang down. The trunks are conspicuously ridged, fluted, and scaly. The needle-like leaves are about ¾"

long, 1/8" wide, and sharp pointed at the tip. They persist on the tree for many years and form flat sprays. The fruit, ⅓" long, is a single, hard, berry-like seed that is embedded, except for the tip, in a coral-red fleshy pulp.
Type locality: Slate Creek, Coffee Creek, Boulder Creek

325. WHITE FIR   PINE FAMILY
Abies concolor   *Pinaceae*
Habitat: with other conifers, 2000'-6000'
The white fir is often associated with the douglas fir but is distinguished from it by the way its needles appear to grow on the stem and by the difference in the cones. The white fir needles often appear to be flattened out into 2 ranks although sometimes they may all turn upward. They never stand out all around the stem as do those of the douglas fir. Unlike the douglas fir, the cones of the white fir, which are 2"-5" long and 1"-1¾" in diameter, stand upright at the ends of the upper branches. The cones also help distinguish the white fir from the red fir when the range of the two firs happens to overlap for they are much smaller. Differences in the needles also separate these two firs. The needles of the white fir are a dark yellowish-green and take on a white tinge as they get older. They are not nearly as stout and stiff as those of the red fir and are usually longer, being ½"-2½" long as contrasted with the ¾"-1¼" length of the red fir needles.
Type locality: Big Flat, Coffee Creek, Boulder Creek

326. RED FIR (tree)   PINE FAMILY
Abies magnifica   *Pinaceae*
Habitat: dry slopes, high elevations

This is the most symmetrical of our conifers. It has blue-green foliage and a reddish-brown bark. There are numerous rigid, horizontal, short branches forming a narrow crown. Its blue-green needles are ¾"-1¼" long, much shorter and stiffer than those of the white fir. Those on the upper branches are bent so that all of the needles appear to be growing from the upper side of the stem in two stiff ranks (see #327). The cones are large, 6"-9" long and up to 3½" in diameter. Unlike other conifers, the cones are never found on the ground. They stand upright on the upper branches where they remain until the scales gradually loosen, break away, and fall to the ground.
Type locality: Horse Haven Meadows, Papoose Lake, Bear Basin

327. RED FIR (needles)   **PINE FAMILY**
Abies magnifica   *Pinaceae*
For description see #326.

328. DOUGLAS FIR   **PINE FAMILY**
Pseudotsuga menziesii   *Pinaceae*
Habitat: moist slopes below 5000'

This is one of the largest of our conifers frequently reaching heights in excess of 200' and diameters of 10'-12'. The smallest branchlets are often drooping. They are evenly covered with short needles which grow at right angles all around the stem giving it a rounded appearance. The douglas fir is not a true fir, the name having been given to it by woodsmen. There are many botanical differences between it and the true firs. The most noticeable difference is the cone which has trident-shaped bracts protruding from between the cone scales. The cones are cinnamon-brown in color, from 2"-3" long and pendulous.
Type locality: Rush Creek, Stuarts Fork, Coffee Creek

329. MOUNTAIN HEMLOCK (cones)   **PINE FAMILY**
Tsuga mertensiana   *Pinaceae*
For description see #330.

330. MOUNTAIN HEMLOCK (tree)   **PINE FAMILY**
Tsuga mertensiana   *Pinaceae*
Habitat: open slopes, higher elevations

This is a graceful tree, 70'-100' tall, with a narrow columnar crown. It usually retains its lowermost branches throughout its life. The slender tip of the tree is soft and nodding making it easy to identify from a distance. Rounded needles are ½"-¾" long, have a small distinct "stem", and cover the branchlets on all sides although they may appear thicker on the upper side. The cones are about 2" long and 1" wide with light brown scales that stand out rigidly at right angles to the axis when open. The cones often hang in dense clusters from the tips of the slender branches, especially near the top of the tree. (See also #329.)
Type locality: Monument Peak, Emerald Lake, Alpine Lake

331. WEEPING SPRUCE
Picea breweriana
Habitat: colder slopes at higher elevations

PINE FAMILY
Pinaceae

This tree has a very limited distribution. It grows to about 75' and has long spreading pendulous lower branches. Growing on these long branches are many "weeping" branchlets that hang straight down for 4'-8'. The needles are ¾"-1" long and grow out from all sides of the stem. They are jointed near the stem on a woody base. When the needles fall this base or "peg" is left behind giving a rough texture to the stem. This "peg" helps distinguish this spruce from any firs that might be associated with it. It has cylindrical cones 3½"-4¼" long and 1¼"-1½" wide.
Type locality: Canyon Creek, Snowslide Lake

332. INCENSE CEDAR
Libocedrus decurrens
Habitat: warm open exposures, under 5000'

CYPRESS FAMILY
Cupressaceae

When young, the contour of the incense cedar is a perfect cone with the lower branches sweeping toward the ground. Old trees have irregular, open, flat tops with huge side branches that turn upwards and grow parallel to the trunk. The trunk tapers rapidly and has a cinnamon-red fibrous bark that is vertically fissured. There are numerous small branchlets from which hang vertical sprays of scale-like leaves. Instead of a conspicuous cone, the cone is small, about 1" long, and consists of 3 pairs of woody scales.
Type locality: Coffee Creek, Stuarts Fork, Weaverville

ILLUSTRATED GLOSSARY

Flower Parts

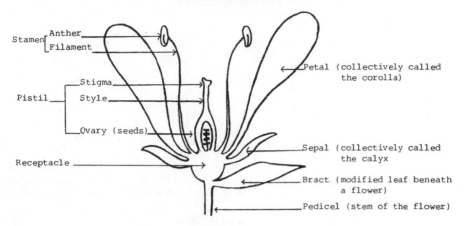

Stamen [Anther
        [Filament

Pistil [Stigma
         Style
         Ovary (seeds)

Receptacle

Petal (collectively called the corolla)

Sepal (collectively called the calyx

Bract (modified leaf beneath a flower)

Pedicel (stem of the flower)

Diagramatic cross-section of a regular flower

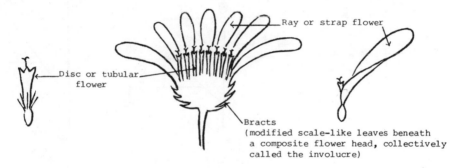

Ray or strap flower

Disc or tubular flower

Bracts
(modified scale-like leaves beneath a composite flower head, collectively called the involucre)

Head of a composite flower

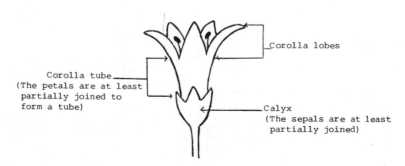

Corolla lobes

Corolla tube
(The petals are at least partially joined to form a tube)

Calyx
(The sepals are at least partially joined)

Tubular flower

185

ILLUSTRATED GLOSSARY

Flower Clusters

A single flower

Head
A compact cluster

Spike
An elongated cluster
of stemless flowers

Raceme
An elongated cluster
of flowers with stems

Panicle
A many branched
cluster

Cyme
A branched cluster
in which the terminal flowers
open first

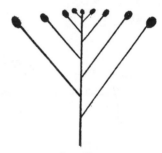

Corymb
A somewhat flat-topped
cluster in which the
outer flowers open first

Umbel
A cluster in which the
stems all originate at
one point

Catkin
A tassellike spike
of small 1-sex flowers
without petals

Whorl
Flowers arranged
in a circle
around a stem

Scorpioid
A one-sided coiled
flower cluster

ILLUSTRATED GLOSSARY
Type and Arrangement of Leaves

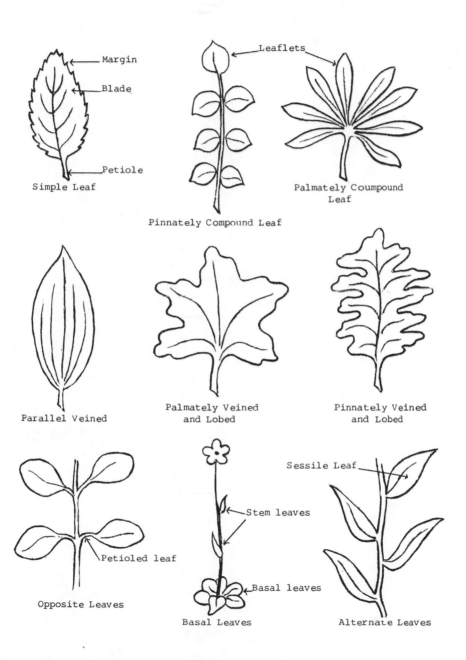

Margin
Blade
Petiole
Simple Leaf

Leaflets
Pinnately Compound Leaf

Palmately Coumpound Leaf

Parallel Veined

Palmately Veined and Lobed

Pinnately Veined and Lobed

Petioled leaf
Opposite Leaves

Stem leaves
Basal leaves
Basal Leaves

Sessile Leaf
Alternate Leaves

INDEX

The numbers following each plant name refer to the species numbers in both the photo and text sections.

NOTES

NOTES

NOTES